A Psimple Psaltery

A Psimple Psaltery:

Building a Bowed Psaltery, From Start to Finish

By Eric Meier

 Sierra's Ascent Publishing

Sierra's Ascent Publishing
PO Box 5543
Hopkins, MN 55343

ISBN 978-0-9822460-0-9

Library of Congress Control Number: 2008911350

A Psimple Psaltery:

Building a Bowed Psaltery, From Start to Finish

Table of Contents

"O God, my heart is fixed; I will sing and give praise, even with my glory. Awake, psaltery and harp: I myself will awake early. I will praise thee, O LORD, among the people: and I will sing praises unto thee among the nations."

—Psalm 108:1-3

An Introduction

Hi, I'm Eric Meier. I build bowed psalteries, and I thought I would share some of my building experience with you. I've designed a project which walks you through the entire process of building this musical instrument—from start to finish.

Why have I taken the time to write this book and share this with you? Because you've got to hear this wonderful instrument in person! It seems that many musical instrument plans consist of an eclectic mix of cardboard, Styrofoam, and celery—but not this one. When you are done, you will have a real, enjoyable, playable, and amazing *musical instrument*. (And your repertoire will not be limited to the four notes of *Mary Had a Little Lamb* either.)

Let me show you what this instrument looks like:

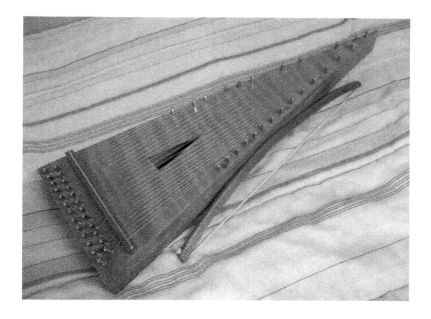

What's not to like about the bowed psaltery? They have the most wonderful ringing sound of any musical instrument that I've ever heard, with a haunting sustain that makes the music seemingly float in midair and tingle in your ears. They are easy to play, and in their most basic form are fairly simple to build. So, welcome!

Welcome to the wonderful of bowed psalteries, that is! That little phrase in the previous paragraph sums up the foundation of this project: *simple to build*. As with any musical instrument, the bowed psaltery can be as simple or extravagant as you want to make it. While the instruments that I build for Phantasy Psalteries (www.phantasypsalteries.com) are a bit more involved, in this book I've created a plan for a *simple* psaltery. By changing the layout and the shape to a basic triangle, and eliminating some of the more intricate steps—along with giving in-depth and thorough directions—I hope to make bowed psalteries available for just about everyone to build.

Everything you need to know to build a bowed psaltery can be found in this book. In order to get a better overview of the instrument itself, I highly recommend you begin by taking a look at the anatomy chart in the next chapter, which points out all the parts and pieces that make up the bowed psaltery.

Have fun, and make some music!

Eric Meier

Let's Build One!

So, you want to build a bowed psaltery? Great! But before we begin, I think it would be a good idea to learn all of the names and terms used for all the parts.

Anatomy of the Bowed Psaltery:

1. Tuning Pins—the pins located at the base of the psaltery. These are the pins that are tightened and loosened to tune the strings. Unlike the hitch pins (#4), these pins are set into a special hardwood pinblock to help ensure that they won't slip or lose their tuning easily.

2. Pinblock (aka wrest plank)—technically the pinblock isn't fully visible in this picture, but is underneath the soundboard. The pinblock is a piece of strong and fine-grained wood (usually hard maple) that holds all of the tuning pins in place.

3. Soundhole—an opening, of many various shapes or sizes, in the top of the soundboard. Think of the soundhole as the mouth of the instrument.

4. Hitch Pins—the pins located along the sides of the psaltery. These pins anchor the strings to the instrument and elevate them above the soundboard. Notes are played by running the bow in between these pins.

5. Bridge—the piece of wood that runs perpendicular across the top of the psaltery. This is the point where the vibrations of the strings are transferred to the instrument's soundboard (#7).

6. Saddle—a piece of metal or hard plastic that runs along the top of the bridge. The saddle's job is to keep the strings from gouging into the wood of the bridge.

7. Soundboard—a thin piece of wood, (usually a quartersawn softwood), that makes up the top of the bowed psaltery. This piece is responsible for transferring the strings' vibrations to the rest of the body of the psaltery.

8. Bow—a simple hardwood bow is pictured above. Bows can be of any number of shapes or sizes. What puts the *bowed* in bowed psaltery.

Items not labeled/included:

For clarity's sake, I have left some items in the picture on the previous page unlabeled. In addition, some features are not present on this particular bowed psaltery. These following items are described below:

- **Strings (unlabeled)**—somewhat self-explanatory; each string wraps overtop the hitch pin, runs across the top of the bridge, and is wound around a corresponding tuning pin at the base of the instrument.

- **Sides (unlabeled)**—along with the pinblock, the sides make up the actual frame of the psaltery. The sides also hold the hitch pins in place. Unlike the tuning pins, which are set in a special pinblock, the hitch pins are stationary, so the sides can be made out of a wider variety of woods.

- **Back (not pictured)**—like the soundboard, the back is also a thin piece of wood. But unlike the soundboard, the back's job is to reverberate the string's vibrations. Think of the back as a tuning fork of sorts.

- **Rose or Rosette (not included)**—any sort of decoration within or around the soundhole. Typically, if it is a pattern or carving *inside* the soundhole, it is considered a *rose*; anything that is inlaid *around* the soundhole is considered a *rosette*. This psaltery has no rose or rosette.

- **Binding (not included)**—the wood trim that runs along the border of the top and/or back of the psaltery. The binding is used to protect the soft edges of the soundboard from dents and dings, as well as seal the end-grain of the wood on the soundboard and back. This psaltery has no binding.

Now that you've got some idea of what all the parts do, and how they come together and interact to make this musical instrument, it's time to take a look at just what we are undertaking to do. Remember, you can always come back to these pages if you forget what something is called.

What we are building is a 25-string bowed psaltery, with a fully chromatic range of just over 2 octaves. By chromatic, I mean that each string goes up in half-step intervals, so we will be able to play all of the sharps and flats in addition to all of the natural notes within the two octaves.

In addition to the actual building, I will also cover the stringing, as well as making a bow for the instrument too. If you would like more information on how a bowed psaltery is actually played, please refer to the corresponding chapter on page 87.

And with that overview, we begin this project! I will be building an actual psaltery right along with you too. (The one pictured on page 3 in the anatomy chart.) The first order of business is to find all of the tools and supplies that we will need to make this project a success.

Good luck!

Tools and Supplies

Alright, before we make some sawdust, we need to get everything ready and make sure we'll have all the needed tools and supplies to finish this project. Most tools listed here will be common to most woodworkers. If you don't have a specific tool, or if you're not a woodworker, you may be able to fudge in a few places, but I would be sure to check the actual building chapters on each item to see if you will be able to improvise something or not.

Some of the woods may require a little bit of extra searching—this isn't like making oak cabinets. Beyond the basic set of tools and woodworking supplies, only a few specialized items are needed; I would say the only two that are an absolute necessity are the zither pins and a tuning wrench to fit them. (See the section on *sources of supplies* on page 124 for more information.)

Here's a listing and a brief description of all the tools and supplies that you'll need to complete this project, along with where to find them in their respective chapter(s):

Tools:

- ³⁄₁₆" **brad-point drill bit**—preferably high quality for accuracy, for drilling the holes for the zither pins. (page 35)
- **Bandsaw or tablesaw**—to cut the 10° miter for the frame, (page 14) and also to generally rip pieces of wood to the correct size.
- **Drill press**—not an absolute necessity, but will definitely help. For drilling the holes for the zither pins. (page 35)
- **Miter saw**—to cut the ends of the pinblock and sides to the correct angles. (pages 13 & 16)
- **High-speed rotary tool (Dremel, B&D wizard, etc.) with cut-off wheel**—for quickly notching the tops of the hitch pins (page 61–62), though a hand-file may also be used.
- **Scrollsaw, jigsaw, or 1⅜" holesaw**—for cutting either a triangular or circular shaped soundhole (page 29) in the top of the psaltery; an exacto knife or similar implement may be used to cut the soundhole manually.

- **Clamps**—various clamps are used in conjunction with jigs to help glue things together as sturdily as possible. I regularly use C-clamps, spring clamps, and bar clamps—along with some shop-made ones as well.
- **Metric and Imperial rulers**—most measurements are given in inches, but some of the more precise measurements dealing with the pin layout (page 32) are given in millimeters (mm).
- **Needle-nose pliers, wire cutters, locking pliers**—used in stringing the psaltery. (page 63)

Materials:

- **Wood glue**—more on the specific types that are most fitting for musical instruments in the glues section of the appendix, (page 100), which is also referenced throughout the building process.
- **Wood finish**—more on the specific types that are most fitting for musical instruments in the varnishing chapter on page 41.
- **Sandpaper, various grits**—used throughout the construction process; hardly seems necessary to mention, but a necessity nonetheless.

Wood: Listed are the approximate dimensions of each piece in rough form; more details as to where to find each piece are given in their respective chapters. In all cases, care should be taken to ensure that the wood is both sound and dry.

- **23" x 8½" x ³⁄₁₆" quartersawn softwood (or plywood)**—soundboard (page 27)
- **23" x 8½" x ³⁄₁₆" hardwood (or plywood)**—back (page 21)
- **23½" x 1½" x ¾" hardwood**—sides (page 12)
- **7¼" x 1½" x 1 ½" hard maple**—pinblock (page 16)
- **7½" x ½" x ½" hardwood**—bridge (page 47)
- **16" x 2" x ³⁄₈" hardwood**—bow (page 82)
- **Various sheet and dimensioned lumber for making jigs**—mainly for the frame (pages 14 & 19)

Hardware: By hardware, I basically mean anything that is part of the psaltery that isn't wood!

- **50 zither pins**—half will be used as the tuning pins, half will be used as the hitch pins; see the sub-section in the chapter on stringing. (page 59)
- **50 feet of music wire**—a total of 25 strings are strung between their respective hitch and tuning pins; see the sub-section in the chapter on stringing. (page 55)
- **⅛" diameter metal/plastic rod, approximately 7¼" long**—this will be the saddle, which will protect the bridge from all the strings. (page 49)

Miscellaneous parts: This is basically everything that is not actually a part of the psaltery, but is still necessary to play or tune it.

- **Tuning wrench**—used to insert all the zither pins and to tune the strings; see the sub-sections within the stringing and tuning chapters. (pages 59 & 74)
- **Bow and rosin**—see the chapter on the bow. (page 77)
- **Digital tuner (optional)**—see the sub-section in the chapter on tuning. (page 70)

The Frame

The frame is probably the most important part of the entire instrument. Between the three pieces of wood, the frame makes up the triangular base of the instrument that holds the load of all the psaltery's strings in tension. It should be well-made and sturdy! Make sure that the pieces fit together cleanly before proceeding to the gluing stage.

Below is a picture of the overall plan of the frame. Please note the 22 15/16" length is for the *overall* length of the instrument, *not* the length of the sides. (Remember, a triangle's *hypotenuse* is longer than its height.)

The Frame

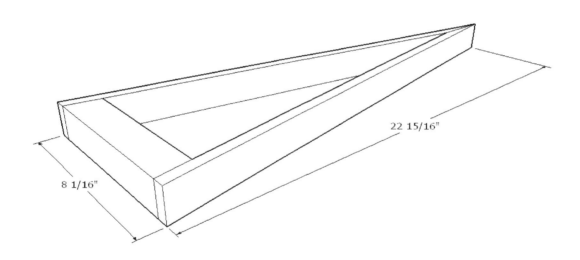

The frame consists of two sides, and the pinblock

Now, you can see from the plan above that you will need two pieces of wood for the sides, and one for the base. This base is actually what all of the tuning pins will be threaded into, and is called the pinblock. The pinblock will be discussed later in this chapter.

The Sides:

For the sides of the instrument, you are free to use virtually any wood available. The sides play a somewhat minor role in how the instrument sounds compared to other areas, but an active role nonetheless. But more than *acoustics*, the sides play a major role in the *weight* of the psaltery.

I mostly use ½" thick sides when I build psalteries to reduce the weight, and also to minimize the amount of vibrations that the sides dampen and deaden. (Compared to a guitar or a violin, a psaltery's sides are big and chunky.) This plan calls for ½" thick sides; however, if you are not careful with your joinery and lumber selection, using sides this thin can compromise the structural strength of your instrument—because some of the glue joints are that much narrower—and you may want to use thicker side pieces.

You are free to use any increased thickness for the sides of your psaltery, keeping in mind that doing so can drastically increase the weight of the instrument. If you are using store-bought wood, it is frequently surfaced to either ¾" or 1" in thickness—this would be fine for use in a psaltery. Some common domestic hardwoods which should be available locally, listed from lightest to heaviest, are: poplar, cherry, soft maple, walnut, birch, hard maple, oak, and hickory.

For more information on this, or for the ever-curious, please take a look at the material density charts I've organized in the appendix beginning on page 120.

Beyond that, there are many, many exotic woods from all over the world to choose from, and many of them are even heavier than the heaviest of the common woods available in the United States. Two interesting stores to peruse locally are Rockler and Woodcraft, both of which have nationwide chains: maybe there is a store near you. Otherwise, feel free to check the yellow pages for woodworking stores or lumberyards in your area.

It is my opinion that a good wood for a first psaltery would be soft maple, which would also color-match the hard maple pinblock fairly well. If you're lucky, you may even be able to find some figured maple that will give dramatic results, such as curly, quilted, or bird's-eye maple. Cherry is also a good choice for beginners.

Now let's take a look at how to process the side pieces so that they can be joined to form the frame:

The Sides

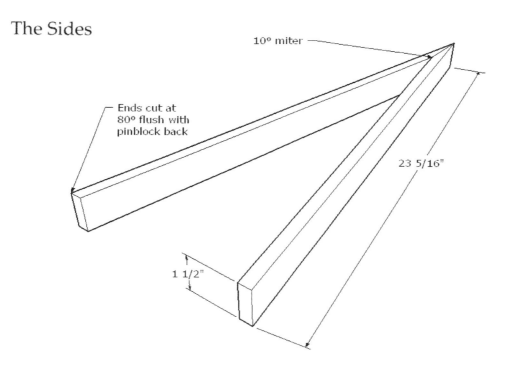

Perhaps the most difficult part of the building is the 10° miter for the tip

The 10° miter joint that forms the tip of the instrument is perhaps one of the hardest aspects of building the psaltery; and we get to do it first thing—what luck! At least we will have it out of the way right away. Now, how do you cut a 10° angle on a board? (*Hint: go try to set your chop saw or miter saw to make an 80° cut.*)

The part that makes this joint hard is the fact that most miter saws will only cut miters up to about 50°. A 10° *miter* cut is usually considered a *taper* cut by most woodworkers, but here it really is a miter cut—two 10° cuts form to make an overall angle of 20° for the tip of the psaltery's frame.

In situations where conventional means can't accomplish a task, a jig is used:

A special jig is used to cut a 10° miter on the side pieces

What you see above is a piece of OSB, (you can use MDF or particleboard too), with little runners attached to the bottom (not visible in picture) that slide in the miter slots of my bandsaw. You can also do the same thing with a tablesaw too—anything that has miter slots running the length of the table. Hardwood or plastic can be used as the runners, but I've found the best option is to use miter slider bars specifically designed for use in jigs, (available in most woodworking stores).

Next, a 10° angle is penciled out on the center of the jig's platform, and a piece of wood is glued or screwed along this line as a fence. (Make sure this board is perfectly square to the platform, or your cuts will be out of square too.) Then, all you have to do is clamp the side pieces, one by one, to the wooden fence piece, and run the entire jig through the saw until the miter is cut. (You only run the jig *halfway* through—don't slice it in half!) Notice the line left by the blade's kerf in the top half of the jig?

Once you cut the miters, save the cutoff scraps for use as gluing shims for the tips, as described on page 20.

Otherwise, an alternative to this miter is to just cut a butt-joint:

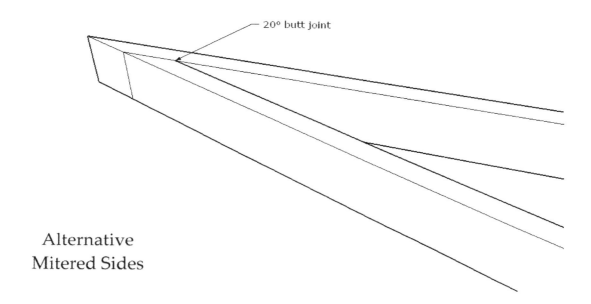

A 20° butt joint may be used in place of the 10° miter joint

To be honest, the butt joint can be every bit as hard as the miter joint. You still have to cut an angle that is beyond the capacity of a miter saw, and is really no easier than a miter, except that you only need to cut one piece instead of two.

The Pinblock:

Now that we have the two side pieces cut, it's time to move on to the third element of the frame: the pinblock.

Depending on how thick your side pieces were, the pinblock may be longer or shorter than what is pictured on the next page. The listed pinblock length (7 ¹⁄₁₆" long) is meant for psalteries with ½" thick sides. Conversely, if you are using thicker sides, you may also leave the pinblock length the same and increase the overall length of the sides instead. (That is to say, do you want the sides to be thicker than the prescribed ½" on the *inside* dimensions of the frame, or the *outside* dimensions.) For simplicity's sake, I'd recommend just shortening the pinblock's length if you've used thicker lumber for the sides.

Here's a quick look at the size of this piece:

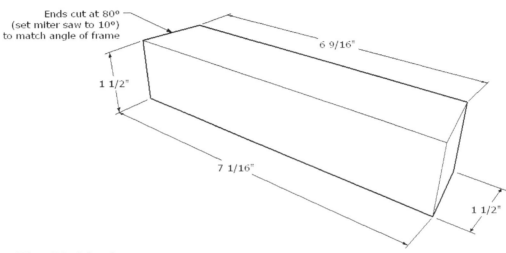

The Pinblock

Unlike the wood used for the sides, the pinblock must be made of a certain kind of wood—usually hard maple. (Well, I shouldn't say *must*, but it's a very good idea.) Basically, the tension of the strings will be held in place by small threaded pins that will be seated in the pinblock. These pins are then rotated either clockwise or counter-clockwise to tighten or loosen the tension on the string—just like a bolt or screw.)

Because the pins are actually threaded into the pinblock, *hard* maple should be used for this piece of the psaltery. If you want to read the entire discussion as to why this is the case, then you can go to the section I've created on pinblock woods in the appendix on page 97. But for those who are just interested in the whats and hows of this project, you can continue on.

You should be able to find hard maple all over the US, either from local sawmills, some hardware stores, woodworking stores such as Rockler or Woodcraft, or from online vendors. And one additional note: although it is best to find one solid piece of maple that is 1½" thick, you are certainly welcome to glue two ¾" thick pieces together to attain the 1½" height—provided the glue joint is clean and solid. (Just make sure the joint runs side to side, and not top to bottom.)

An important note regarding the selection of pinblock wood: you want it plain. When you are looking at hard maple, do not choose a piece that has knots, curl, spalt, bird's-eye, or anything out of the ordinary. The crucial thing to remember is *consistency* and *homogeny*. Pinblocks have a thankless job—to hold the tuning pins still, and therefore keep the strings in tune. Using a "wild" piece of wood for this area will make it harder to keep the psaltery in tune. (But even though the pinblock is made of hard maple, you can still cover the exposed back side with a thin strip of wood that matches the wood used for the sides to give the frame a more consistent, uninterrupted look.)

In my demonstration psaltery, I have used an exotic hardwood called Kwila for the sides, and a hard maple pinblock. (I later added a thin veneer slice of Kwila to cover the maple pinblock at the base of the psaltery.)

A loose layout of the psaltery's frame, still unglued

Gluing the Frame Together:

Once all of the pieces have been cut and test fit, it's time to glue the frame together. One item should be mentioned on the test fitting: make sure the pinblock fits snugly against the sides. The bond between the pinblock and the sides is probably the most important joint of the entire instrument, and is subject to the greatest amount of stress. If nothing else, try to get this area as clean and snug fitting as possible.

Now, it's true that there are all kinds of woodworking glues available, but some are better than others when it comes to musical instrument building. While it's possible to use regular yellow wood glue, I would recommend taking a look at the section in the appendix discussing various glues and their strengths and weaknesses, found on page 100. For beginners, I would actually recommend using some 2-part woodworker's epoxy.

Gluing the frame together is much trickier than it looks. The reason for this is because when you go to clamp the sides against the pinblock, it will want slide out like a banana peel! (And if the psaltery could laugh at you, it probably would right about now.)

There are probably a hundred ways to go about doing this job, but the most important part is that you have a plan *before* you start slopping glue on your carefully cut pieces.

What I use is a simple jig to hold the pieces in place, which also gives you a place to clamp the wood so it won't move around. It may seem like a lot of jigs are used in this chapter, but they really help give better results. (Once you have a bunch of glue slathered on the wood, and you're quickly struggling to keep the psaltery's parts together without sliding apart, you'll realize why you needed a plan *before* jumping into gluing—*sans* any sort of jig.)

The jig pictured on the following page is simply a piece of particleboard slightly bigger than the overall size of the psaltery, with the overall outline of the frame carefully measured and penciled onto the jig's base. (Take care to get the narrow angle at the tip laid out accurately.)

A simple jig is used to ensure that the pinblock stays put during glue-up

Pieces of wood are glued or screwed down onto the jig's base along the lines marked out for the sides and back (again making sure these pieces are square and level.) These glued pieces of wood sit on top of the jig's platform and hold the psaltery's frame in place while being glued. (They also act as an excellent place to position clamps to keep the frame from sliding around.)

I gave myself about 2" of extra room on the bottom guide piece that holds the pinblock so I wouldn't have to be absolutely perfect on the overall length of the psaltery. I then use a flat and level strip of wood to hold the pinblock snug up against the side pieces, and pound regular wooden door/window shims in between this wood strip and the bottom guide-block on the jig to make up the extra distance. (*Note: I also use either waxed paper or plastic cling wrap between the psaltery and the jig to prevent the instrument from being glued to the jig.*)

From here, you can clamp the sides against the pinblock with a bar clamp as tight as you want—it's not going anywhere! Also, you should be able to get enough clamping force at the tip of the psaltery with just one or two spring clamps; but I like to overdo things sometimes, so I used 10° shims that match the complementary angle of the tip to really clamp down hard with a C-clamp.

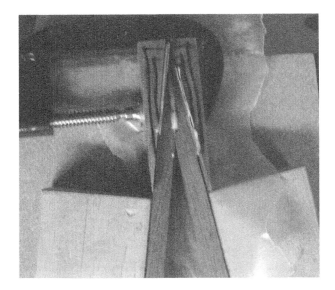

10° shims are used to give the C-clamp an even clamping surface on the tip

This is where the cutoff scraps from the 10° miter cuts mentioned at the top of page 15 will come in handy. Since they were cut from the same board, and are at the same angle, they are guaranteed to fit. (I sometimes have to wedge some sandpaper between the shim and the frame to prevent the shim from sliding around.)

Once you have glued up the frame for the instrument, give yourself a pat on the back: one of the most important steps is finished. It's (mostly) all downhill from here, except possibly for the final stringing. But more on that later, for now we move our attention to the psaltery's back.

The Back

Compared to the frame, the back is much easier to fit. The only thing that may be of trouble is the *thickness* of wood required—between ³⁄₁₆" to ⅛".

Here is a sketch of the overall dimensions of the back:

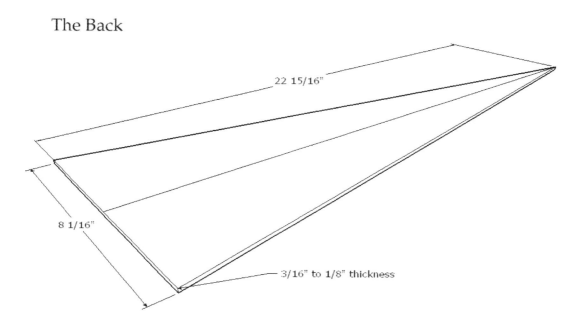

The Back

22 15/16"

8 1/16"

3/16" to 1/8" thickness

The only difficult part of sizing the back is finding lumber that is thin enough

It should be noted that the sizes listed for the back are the *exact* size—I would recommend giving yourself at least an extra ⅛" on all sides as slop room. Personally, I first build the frame, and then just lay the frame directly on top of the back and trace the outline. (That's why I have the frame listed *first* in the order of construction.)

Now, there are several ways to get the back down to the required thickness. The first and easiest is just to buy ⅛" thick plywood; it's most commonly available as *⅛" Baltic birch plywood*. Plywood this thin isn't always available at hardware stores, but can usually be found at most woodworking and hobby stores; if you live in the United States, you can check locally for Rockler or Woodcraft, both of which have nationwide chains.

In addition to ⅛" plywood, a lot of woodworking and hobby stores also sell certain species of solid wood down to ⅛" thick. This is sometimes referred to as "craft wood." However, you are probably not going to find such pieces wide enough, (about 8 ¼" total width), so it may be necessary to edge-glue two or three pieces together to get to the required width. (Note the line running down the middle of the back in the drawing on page 21. The plans show a two-piece back, which is what I have used on the psaltery for this project as well.)

There are also many more vendors online, especially on eBay, which sell wood in 3⁄16" and ⅛" thicknesses. You can try searching for guitar backs as well, (usually found under the search term *guitar sets*), which are sometimes wide enough to be used as a one-piece psaltery back. Basically, guitar backs come in two halves, which are meant to be edge-glued together to form the back of a guitar, and one half should be ample to cover the back of a much smaller psaltery. Just be sure that the backs are both long enough and wide enough before ordering! Most backs will not be 23" long, so you may have to look around.

Another option is to find a board the right size in length and width, and plane it down to the right thickness. If you have a thickness planer, this might be a good way to use a wider selection of woods for the back, though it is a bit wasteful. You could also plane the board down to the right thickness by hand using a bench plane—though if you are not proficient with hand planes, this could prove to be a very tedious and time-consuming task!

Otherwise, a thickness sander will also do an excellent job at thicknessing the back, but is probably not a common tool to most home woodworkers. There is, however, one other way to get down to the right thickness with what is arguably the most versatile of a luthier's power tools: a bandsaw.

For the back of the demonstration psaltery on this project, I resawed matching Kwila panels from the same board as the sides using a bandsaw. If you have a bandsaw with enough resaw capacity, you can slice your own backs from solid lumber. I prefer to bookmatch my backs so that the grain pattern is symmetrical on both halves. Resawing is probably the most versatile and economical method, but it does require a saw with both a good resaw blade, and also a sufficiently tall resaw height. (Over 4" of clearance from the table to the blade guard for two-piece backs, and over 8" of clearance for single-piece backs.)

A Note Regarding the Thickness of the Back:

I list a range of thicknesses—from ³⁄₁₆" down to ⅛"—because a lot will depend on what woods are used, and how comfortable you are working with wood this thin. I would say with plywood you can definitely use ⅛" thickness, (and probably even thinner), without any worries because its cross-grain plies give it a lot of strength. But if this is your first time, and you are concerned with the consistency of the wood, you can leave the back at ³⁄₁₆" thick.

I wouldn't recommend having a back that is much thicker than this, as it will muffle and absorb a lot of the instrument's vibrations. The back's job is *reverberate* the sounds of the strings—similar to that of a tuning fork. Plywood is not as good at doing this as a solid-wood back, because the grain of each layer of plywood runs perpendicular to each ply next to it. Additionally, there is a lot of glue needed to bond the plies together, which can also inhibit the path of the vibrations. (Not to mention that some plywood can just have junk-wood for the core, with nicer, sanded wood for the outer plies.)

But, with all this said, if this is your first and only bowed psaltery, then a lot of this will really make little difference as you won't know the difference anyway. The instrument you build will be your best bowed psaltery ever! (But also your only one too.)

Gluing the Back to the Frame:

Once you have the back cut out and thicknessed properly, it is time to glue it to the frame of the psaltery. Because the back serves to reinforce the frame, I like to use creep-resistant glue for gluing the back on, just like the glue that was used for the frame.

If you haven't already, now would be a good time to have a look at the various glues used in musical instrument construction found in the appendix on page 100.

Gluing the back on does not require the use of any jigs or special tools. You can accomplish the gluing with an array of clamps. I think on my first bowed psaltery, I used just about every clamp I owned to glue/fight the back on, which was quite a hodge-podge team of clamps—"*emptied the bench*," as they say in baseball.

Nowadays, I glue backs on with a clamping fixture called a go-bar deck. It certainly isn't necessary to use one of these, but they sure do make the gluing process a lot more refined and pleasant. Here's a picture of the deck that I use:

A go-bar deck was used to glue the Kwila back onto the frame of the psaltery

Basically, a go-bar deck consists of a sturdy table with an enclosed top. Then, the work is placed on the base of the table—called the deck—and strips of wood, (I use dowels), all of identical length are wedged between the ceiling and the object to be glued. These are the go-bars. (I also use a thin piece of acrylic cut into a triangular psaltery shape to protect the psaltery from being gouged by the dowels.)

Most other go-bar decks that I've seen use all-thread rods for the four legs, and have an adjustable ceiling. I chose to build a sturdy stationary version with solid 2x4 lumber for the legs and reinforced the deck and ceiling with 2x3s. Otherwise, I find that I get some warping and bowing when I start wedging all the dowels in place. I just use sheets of MDF, plywood, or hardboard as spacers to bring the instrument up to the correct height, rather than have the table itself adjustable.

The nice thing about the go-bar deck is that it lets you put pressure *exactly* where you need it. You are not limited to just the edges, but you can get deep in the body of the psaltery—especially over the pinblock—to make sure every square inch of the psaltery is firmly glued down. (I actually added a few more dowels after the picture on page 24 was taken.)

Clean-up and Labeling:

Once the back has been glued on, I like to scrape or chisel off all the glue squeeze-out that has formed on the inside of the psaltery. This is the main reason why we have chosen to glue the back on *before* the top. Otherwise, you can see the glue along the edges when you look through the soundhole in the top.

An electric wood-burning pen was used to label the inside of this psaltery

One other thing that you might want to consider before you move on to attaching the top is putting a label of some sort on the inside of the instrument: your name, when or where the instrument was made, along with any other relevant information that might be of help to others if you ever give it away to someone. If you label the instrument about a third the way up on the inside back of the instrument, it will be visible when you peer through the soundhole.

You can glue in a paper label, carve something, burn it in, write it with ink—some people even inlay their signatures with wood or mother of pearl. If you plan to keep your instrument around for a while, a label will be helpful.

The Soundboard

It should come as little surprise that the top is of exactly the same dimensions as the back. However, since the top serves a much different purpose than the back, it accordingly should be made of different woods. As a reminder, here's the size of the top, which is no different than the back:

The Top

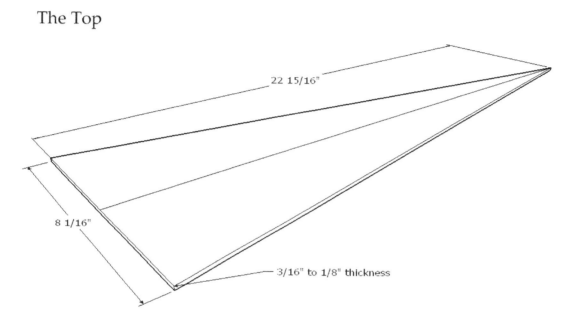

22 15/16"

8 1/16"

3/16" to 1/8" thickness

The top is the same dimensions as the back, but should be of a quartersawn softwood

Again, I felt in order to keep the actual sections on building separate from the explanation sections, I have put the reasoning behind the type of soundboard woods in the appendix on page 104. If you only want to know the whats and hows of building a bowed psaltery, you can continue on to the next section.

Sources of Soundboards:

Finding a soundboard can be as easy as simply using a ⅛" thick piece of plywood—just as was done for the back. The cross-plies in plywood help give it enough strength, but acoustically it can stifle the strings' vibrations. Like any aspect of this project, if this is your first time, you can use almost anything, and you probably won't be able to tell the difference anyway.

However, I would recommend using an appropriate solid-wood top for the soundboard. You may have to buy this online, or you could find a gem at your local lumber yard if you know what to look for. There are many sources for quartersawn instrument tops, but one difficulty is finding one that is 23" long. Acoustic guitar tops are a good place to start if hunting online, (one guitar top will have enough wood for two, possibly even three or four bowed psaltery tops), just make sure that the size is big enough before ordering.

If you are able to resaw lumber up to 4", or you have a thickness planer, you may be able to find some good boards that can be made into tops at the local lumberyard or woodworking store. Just look for a board that has vertical rings (quartersawn) and is clear and completely free of knots. (Also avoid using the center core of the tree—sometimes called the pith— which is very unstable.) The board you chose should have growth rings spaced as closely together as possible to give it more stiffness and strength. I would generally say no more than ~3/16" between growth rings. To bring the soundboard down to the right thickness, you can use any one of the methods listed in the previous chapter on pages 21–23 discussing the back.

For the psaltery in this project, I was able to find some nice curly redwood boards locally. After scrounging through *the entire pile of wood*, I found maybe two or three boards that were suitable to be sawn up into soundboards. I bought one of the boards and resawed it into about three or four tops. The board was also wide enough (8"+ wide) for a one-piece top too. (You can edge-glue a two-piece top if needed—it should still be as strong as a single piece if done correctly. I just use *Titebond Original* for this gluing task.)

The Soundhole:

Now that we have the soundboard dimensioned to the right size and shape, we just have one last thing to do to it before we glue it to the frame and finish out the soundbox of the psaltery. We need to cut a big hole in it! This "big hole" is actually called the *soundhole.* Basically, it's where the sound comes out. I think of the soundhole as the mouth of the instrument. The soundhole has a lot of flexibility in terms of its shape and location. Basically, any opening (or openings) of the right surface area will work.

In my plans, keeping with the simple theme, I have chosen to use a basic triangle of roughly the same ratio as the overall dimensions of the psaltery (3:1) for the soundhole. Here's the plan:

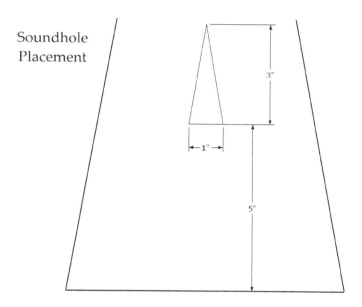

The soundhole pattern above can actually be cut by hand with an exacto knife, repeatedly scoring the soft wood of the top. A scroll saw or jigsaw would also be great, and you could even cut patterns in the top instead of a triangle. Or, you could even drill an array of smaller holes in patterns or in various locations on the top—so long as the total surface area is equal to the triangle's area.

For those curious, the triangle shown above has an area of 1.5 square inches. If you just want to drill a big hole using a holesaw, a 1⅜" diameter circle would closely match the area of the triangle. For those wondering how I arrived at these numbers, and the sizing of soundholes in general, you can take a slight detour to the section on soundhole sizing in the appendix found on page 107.

Another common soundhole style is gluing in a laser-cut rose. Basically, you can buy a small circular piece of plywood that has been cut into intricate patterns by a laser. You then drill a hole in your soundboard and glue the rosette to either the top or underside of the soundboard, or even mount it flush, provided you drill a hole of the exact size. Roses are available from various locations online, such as Musicmaker's (www.harpkit.com) and Folkcraft (www.folkcraft.com).

Once you have everything set just the way you want it, glue the soundboard to the frame, just as you did with the back. Take extra care to make sure that the area around the pinblock and corners are securely glued to the frame, as this will go a long way in reinforcing the strength of the instrument.

Just to catch up on where we are on this project, here is a picture of my psaltery as it's progressing:

The rough soundbox, with a curly redwood top, all glued together

You can see I left extra space around the rim of the instrument so I wouldn't come up short! I will use a router with a flush-trim bit and then some sandpaper to clean everything up and get it looking nice and tidy.

Now that everything has been glued together, do any necessary sanding or scraping to get your psaltery looking and feeling smooth; but keep the upper edges/corners of the soundboard crisp, and don't round them over yet. In the next chapter we'll be using the top edge of the psaltery as a reference point for the layout of the pins.

Pin Layout

Now that we have the main component of the psaltery built, (sometimes called the soundbox), we can begin to lay out the positioning of the zither pins. In this category, there are two locations for the pins: the first group is the *tuning* pins, which are embedded into the pinblock at the base of the psaltery, and the second group, (whose spacing is much more critical), is the *hitch* pins—where each string will eventually be anchored along the sides of the psaltery.

The Layout of the Tuning Pins:

We'll start with the easiest group—the tuning pins. There will be two rows of pins, with 13 pins on the bottom row, and 12 pins on the top row, all equally spaced, for a total of 25 tuning pins. The first step is to divide the pinblock up into three sections. The bottom row starts ⅜" up from the bottom of the psaltery, with ½" dividing the two rows. See the plan below:

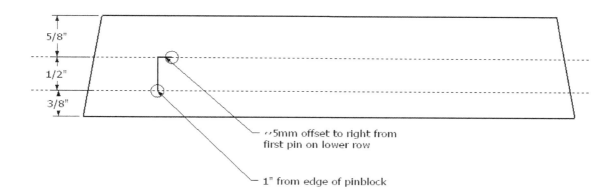

Pinblock Row
  Spacing

Start laying things out by lightly drawing two pencil lines across the top of the psaltery, with the first line being ⅜" up from the base of the psaltery. (These lines will obviously be erased or sanded off prior to finishing.) Then, measure up ½" and draw the line for the second row.

Next, looking at the drawing on the previous page, imagine that you can see through your psaltery's top with x-ray vision, and you can see the hard maple beneath. The first pin on the bottom row starts 1" from the edge of the pinblock. Please note, this does *not* mean 1" from the edge of the instrument; depending on how thick you made your sides, this distance will vary; with ½" sides, the first pin should be located a little over 1½" in from the left edge.

Next, move from the location of the first pin on the lower row upward to the second row, and measure over to the right about 5mm. This point is where the first pin of the upper row will be. This 5mm distance offsets the pins on the top row so they don't completely block the string's path to the back row.

Now, continuing on, measure out 13 pins for the bottom row, and 12 pins for the upper row. The plan below shows the spacing on the standard sized pinblock we have been using according to the plans.

Tuning Pin
Spacing

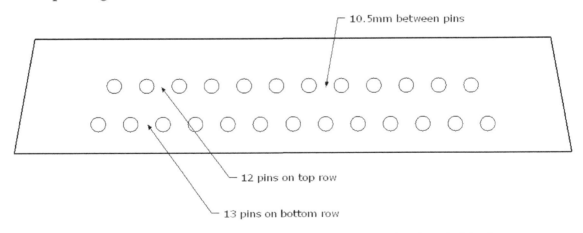

25 pins are spaced evenly across two rows in the pinblock

You may need to adjust your spacing to get the pins centered on the pinblock and looking right. Obviously you won't be able to measure over and count exactly half of a millimeter, but if you put a ruler along the line, you can count 10.5mm, then 21mm, then 31.5mm, and so on. Doing so prevents tiny errors from accumulating and throwing off the last few pins. ½mm × 12 = 6mm, so your spacing could be off by as much as ¼" or more by the end of the pinblock, which can be significant.

> *(Note: You may notice in some photos that the project psaltery has the tuning pins flared out a bit more at the base than what the plans call for. When building the demonstration psaltery, I found that the strings came very close to overlapping on some of the hitch pins, and decided to alter the plans by compressing the tuning pins in toward the center of the pinblock to alleviate the string spacing. With the revised spacing, the strings should travel almost straight down from the hitch pins to the tuning pins.)*

The Layout of the Hitch Pins:

Of all the measurements on a bowed psaltery, perhaps none is more important than the spacing of the hitch pins. It is the hitch pins that determine the vibrating length of the string, and therefore the tension on the string, how close it is to its breaking point, and to a great extent, how nice the string will sound overall. Take your time with this step, and make sure you measure as accurately as possible.

Now, to begin laying out the hitch pins, we will first draw two lines on the soundboard, one down each side of the psaltery. (Again, we will erase or sand off these lines later.) Measure in exactly ¼" from the right edge of the psaltery at several points along the length of the instrument, and pencil in a dot or hash mark at each point; then connect these dots, making sure that the line is parallel to the side of the psaltery. Repeat this for the left side of the psaltery.

Where the two lines meet at the tip is the first note. This is where the first hitch pin hole will be drilled, and this is the base from which all the other pins are positioned.

Look at the spacing for the remaining 24 pins on the following page:

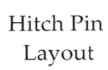

Hitch Pin Layout

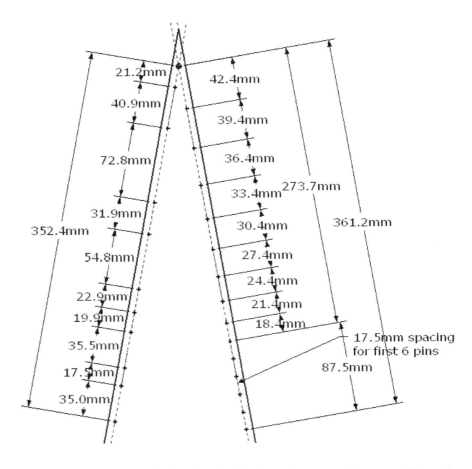

Take great care to accurately lay out all the hitch pin locations on the soundboard

Again, you are not expected to be able to eyeball and measure out a tenth of a millimeter, but the numbers are included to avoid *cumulative* errors. If I were to round off all of the distances, the cumulative effect at the end would be off by a significant margin. You can check your overall spacing by measuring the very last pin on each side and seeing if it's within 1 or 2 millimeters of 361.2mm for the right, and 352.4mm for the left.

Better yet, simply put a metric ruler down the entire length of the side, and add up each number successively to eliminate the chance for a cumulative error. Alternatively, you could simply measure out the first and last pins, and then work your way inward from each end, halving the cumulative effect.

The right-hand side is the most straightforward. If you look at the bottom right of the plan, the first 6 pins have equal spacing of 17.5mm each. From there, the spacing is 18.4mm, and increases by 3mm on each successive pin, up to 42.4mm spacing. If you are curious as to why this is so, I've included a side-discussion in the appendix on page 114 talking about string lengths and hitch pin spacing on the bowed psaltery.

Notice that the pins on the left-hand side are arranged like the black keys on a piano. (They are the sharps and flats.) They occur in a two-three, two-three pattern. (Except the first sharp and the last two sharps are outside of the range of the psaltery, so it's: two, two-three, two-one.) Don't be alarmed if it appears that there are gaps in the pins on the left-hand side— there's no such thing as B-sharp or E-sharp.

Drilling the Holes for the Pins:

Once you have everything laid out, look everything over once more to make sure that there are no obvious errors or mistakes. Once you've drilled a hole in the top, it's hard to un-drill! Now begin by drilling ³⁄₁₆" diameter holes in all the hitch pin locations.

As for the depth of each hole, I personally drill about as deep as I possibly can without risking the bit piercing through to the other side. In all practicality, about 1¼" deep should be fine. However, I am a big fan of "trimming the fat" so to speak, and the sides of a bowed psaltery— compared to most other stringed instruments—are thick and blocky. Any opportunity where I can eliminate unneeded material and improve sound transmission across the instrument will be taken. So, whenever possible, I drill as deep as I can—within safe limits of course.

For the actual drilling, I recommend using a high-quality brad-point drill bit and a drill press. A brad-point bit is a drill bit with a tiny spur (brad) at the tip to help keep the bit from wandering and to ensure that you know exactly where the hole is going to be drilled. Also, higher quality bits are machined to much tighter tolerances and will be surer to be at exactly ³⁄₁₆". (Chances are, if you pulled the bit from a 101 piece set from China, it is suspect at best.) Put the bit in the chuck and spin it, and focus on the very tip of the brad point: if it visibly wobbles much at all, I wouldn't use it.

³⁄₁₆" brad point bits, from left to right: carbide tipped, high speed steel, and a generic

I have been using a carbide-tipped brad point bit, (see picture above, on the left), and I love it. This may be overkill for just one psaltery, but for me, it's worth its weight in gold. I bought it from Lee Valley (www.leevalley.com). The middle bit is a high-quality steel bit made in Germany, and the one on the far right is a junk bit that is from an old drill bit set. Quality bits can be found at woodworking stores, and for a bit this small, the cost should be minimal.

The whole point of this discussion is that the actual zither pins used for the psaltery—especially those used as the tuning pins—rely on very shallow threads to hold themselves in the wood. If the hole is drilled too big, (which can easily happen with a wobbly bit), it can adversely effect how well the pins' threads bite into the pinblock, resulting in a decrease of tuning stability. It would be a good idea to drill a hole in a piece of scrap wood and see how snugly the pin can be threaded into the wood. For the highest stability in tuning, you want it very snug—these pins are precisely made for a ³⁄₁₆" hole.

One last optional tip when drilling is to tilt the drill press table 15° sideways when drilling the holes for the *tuning* pins. The reason for this is because when you are winding the music wire onto the tuning pins for the first time, the string will want to wander up and down the tuning pin. By setting the tuning pins back at a 15° angle, it is much easier to wind the wire onto the pin downward. By tilting the holes, you will save yourself a lot of time during the stringing phase, which to me is much more tedious than the hole-drilling phase!

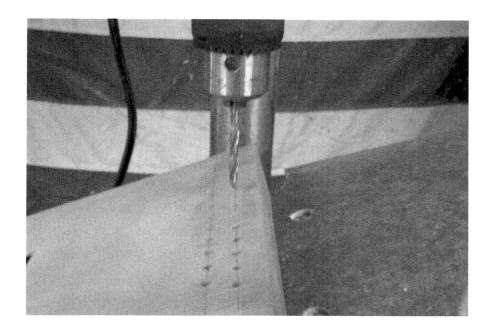

The table of the drill press is tilted 15° to drill the holes for the tuning pins

Installing Optional Note Markers:

One more thing that is common to find on bowed psalteries is the presence of note markers, (very similar to fret markers found on a guitar).

Each builder seems to have their own system or method of doing this, but the overall goal is to make playing the bowed psaltery easier.

Usually a dot is inlaid between two hitch pins to emphasize certain strings. Look at the picture of the demonstration psaltery on the next page for a better idea:

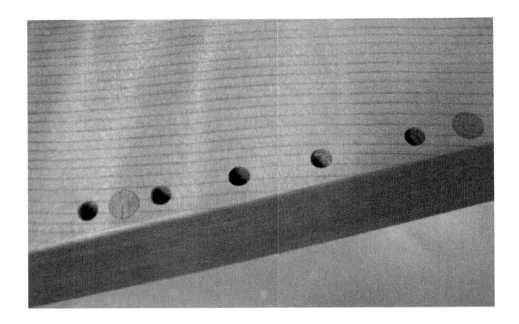

¼ " wooden plugs are inlaid flush to mark the locations of specific notes

On this current psaltery, I chose to use wooden markers cut from scrap lumber with a plug cutter. On the left, you can see a ¼" diameter Kwila dot, (it matches the side and back wood), and just barely visible on the far right is a dot made of Bloodwood. My standard procedure is to mark all the C-notes with one color, and all the F-notes with another color. I choose to only mark the right-hand side, as the irregular spacing on the left side is enough for me to get my bearings quickly when playing.

It's up to you as to which notes to mark, and how you want to mark them. You can view the chapter on tuning on page 69 to help you determine where to place them, and what notes you may want to mark. (Most people will at least mark the C-notes, and usually either the G or F notes as well.) Just remember that in order to mark the C-notes, find all the strings/pins that are tuned to C on the tuning chart, and put a marker *below* that pin, not *above* it.

On some of my fancier bowed psalteries, I have used mother of pearl, and even gemstones to mark the notes. For a *simple* psaltery, however, you can just use a ⅛", ³⁄₁₆" or ¼" diameter wooden dowel: inserted, glued, cut off, and sanded flush with the soundboard. Or, you can buy a ¼" plug cutter and cut your own plugs from any kind of wood you want. One advantage to this method is that a plug cutter will cut face-grain plugs, whereas a dowel will result in end-grain note markers.

Plug cutters are available at most hardware stores for a modest price— usually between $5 and $10. Otherwise, you can find higher-quality plug cutters from local woodworking stores.

A ¼" plug cutter is used to make custom wooden note markers

Once you have all the pin locations marked and drilled, and any note markers inlaid, sand off or erase any remaining layout lines and get the entire instrument smooth and clean. Also, go over any sharp edges and corners and dull them down with sandpaper.

Round over and smooth out the front tip, the top and bottom edges of the body, and the side corners at the base. In general, make the instrument comfortable to hold, and sanded smooth in preparation for applying a finish.

Start with either 80 or 120 grit sandpaper for this step, depending on how much work the psaltery needs. (The edges can be rounded down much faster by using coarse grit sandpaper.) From there, work your way up the grits until you've reached a satisfactory smoothness; in most cases, this stopping point is usually around 180 or 220 grit.

Also, if you've used an open-pored wood for the back and sides, such as Walnut or Mahogany, you might want to consider using a pore-filler before applying a finish. Pore-fillers are simply used to give the wood a smoother, more uniform surface—they're used solely for cosmetic benefit. Not to be confused with wood putty, pore-fillers are usually available in a paste form, and can be found at most woodworking stores.

There are both water-based and oil-based pore-fillers, in varying shades and colors, (and even transparent), and each one can require a different technique or tool to apply. Always follow the manufacturer's instructions that are specific to the pore-filler that you're using for the best results.

Varnishing

Different builders will begin finishing their instruments at different times, and during different stages of construction. Personally, I like to finish the instrument *before* I add the bridge, but *after* I drill the holes for the pins. I do it *before* the bridge is added because it is much easier to apply and sand the finish without the protuberance of the bridge blocking me; and I do it *after* the holes for the pins are drilled because the bit can sometimes mar the finish if you are not careful. Also, there is all the commotion on the table of the drill press—with the wood chips of 50 drilled holes flying everywhere—that is likely to scratch and rough up the finish. (Not to mention that you have to know where the hitch pins are in order to inlay the note markers.)

But *when* to apply the finish will also depend on the *type* of finish used as well. If it is a simple oil finish, it probably won't make too much of a difference either way. But if a thicker film-building finish is used, you may want to apply the finish *before* drilling the holes for the pins to avoid getting "finish gunk" in the holes. (Or at the very least, clean the holes out with the bit after the finish has dried.) This is especially important for the tuning pin holes, which should be clean and free from debris or residue to make tuning easier.

Considering the Attributes of a Finish:

Choosing a finish for a musical instrument brings up a lot of the same issues that we have encountered when we were choosing a glue—the things that work for common woodworking tasks may not be ideal for instruments. Because of the huge surface area of the finish, especially on the critical soundboard area, one important question arises when considering finishes—one that never comes up with other woodworking projects:

Will this finish inhibit the strings' vibrations as they travel across the wood?

Acoustic dampening is typically considered the primary concern with musical instrument finishes, and secondarily comes either durability, or beauty.

Dampening is the primary concern, and this is caused mainly by two things: the *hardness* of the finish, and the *thickness* of the finish. What we are really after is a finish that affects the sound as little as possible, (yet still protects and beautifies the wood.) This is commonly called *acoustic transparency*.

Hardness affects the acoustics because a finish that is hard—rather than soft or flexible—will have a less noticeable dampening of the strings' vibrations. Related to this is of course how thick the finish is built up on the instrument. If a thick, heavy coating is present on the soundboard, it will also absorb a lot of the vibrations and keep them from reaching the rest of the instrument. (This is most apparent when paint is used as a finish.)

Taking into account the hardness of the finish, many woodworkers will immediately think of polyurethane: after all, it is frequently touted as one of the hardest, and most durable of all wood finishes. However, all the claims are simply based on a confusion of terms: we equate a finish's resistance to be scratched with its hardness.

Polyurethane is actually flexible and elastic, which is what helps to give it a high resistance to scratching. However, this means that polyurethane can have a high dampening effect on the instrument, which is not what we are after acoustically. And not only that, but it tends to be much thicker than most finishes, so it builds up heavier layers on the instrument—compounding the problem.

What we are after is mainly a finish that is *brittle*. While most finishes that are truly "hard" do not have quite the same scratch resistance as polyurethane, they are superior in terms of acoustics—and with proper care, many have acceptable durability anyway. This isn't a hardwood floor you're walking on!—it's not even a rowdy rock guitar, it's a *bowed psaltery*.

Also, if a finish is not *brittle*, it may be able to make up for it acoustically by instead being *thin*. Though with thinner finishes—usually ones that do not build up a film finish on top of the instrument—durability can be compromised. On the upside, they are usually also easy to repair.

The most acoustically transparent finishes are those that are both *hard* and *thin*.

So, now that we've gotten a little bit clearer understanding as to what things to look for in a finish, it's time to look at what options are available that fit these criteria:

Finishing Options for Musical Instruments:

- **Lacquer**—Probably among the most common of finishes used for musical instruments. It dries hard, (and quickly), and can be sprayed on—either with dedicated HVLP spray equipment in a spray booth, or simply from store-bought spray cans. Regular nitro-cellulose lacquer spray cans are widely available at nearly all hardware, woodworking, and even general stores. One noted item with lacquer is that it can yellow over time—which can be considered desirable on darker woods; on lighter woods—not so much. But *"yellowing"* sounds bad, so we'll just call it *"aging."*

- **Shellac**—Another common choice for musical instruments is shellac. Shellac can really give mixed results because of one big drawback: once shellac is mixed, it has a relatively short shelf-life. Accordingly, a lot of the pre-mixed shellac that you buy off the shelf can give poor results because it has been sitting in a store for months—if not years. By "poor results" I mean it will remain somewhat soft and won't fully harden. However, *freshly mixed shellac*, made from shellac flakes and denatured alcohol, is both hard and relatively durable, and makes an excellent choice as an instrument finish; shellac flakes can be found at most woodworking stores. (This was the finish used on the bowed psaltery for this book.)

- **Tung Oil**—Tung oil is a fairly broad and somewhat vague term. When sold as 100% raw tung oil, it tends to be soft and does not build up much of a film on the wood; but its advantage is that it is very easy to apply. You simply wipe it on, and wipe the excess off. However, tung oil can also be cooked to help it dry faster and harder, (called polymerization), which allows the finish to build up a protective film on the wood surface. This type of finish tends to be harder and more durable than raw tung oil. Lastly, tung oil can darken with age, but usually not as much as linseed oil or lacquer. Various blends and mixes of tung oil are commonly available at hardware and woodworking stores.

- **Boiled Linseed Oil**—Very similar to tung oil in acoustic properties, linseed oil is also an easy-to-apply, wipe-on oil finish. In the past, linseed oil has been cooked or boiled to alter the oil, which allows the oil to dry much faster and harder. Nowadays, "boiled" linseed oil is not actually boiled at all, but instead chemical driers are added to the raw linseed oil to help the finish fully harden—achieving the same effect as boiling. Regular boiled linseed oil is available at most hardware and woodworking stores. Another choice that has become available is *Tried and True Oil*, which is a truly "boiled" linseed oil, (or at the very least, cooked). Because it doesn't have any of the added chemical driers, it is completely non-toxic, even in its uncured state—an unheard-of rarity with wood finishing products. This finish is available from Woodcraft and Lee Valley. (Try to look for a store location locally, and get the *Varnish Oil* variety of the oil.)

- **Varnish Oils**—This is another very broad and vague term, and encompasses any oil-based varnish. Manufacturers will use just about any name they can think of to get you to buy their products (i.e., teak oil, danish oil, rejuvenation oil, etc.) Some work better than others, but some general rules of thumb can be followed: see if it can be built up to a film finish, or if it is simply rubbed into the wood. Finishes that are only rubbed into the wood tend to be softer, and offer less protection than film-building finishes. They will often emphasize that they are water-resistant, (since when do you get musical instruments wet?) and will sidestep their durability. This is because the finish is *in* the wood, not *on* it. (A bullet-proof vest doesn't do you a lot of good if it's *in* you, does it?) One well-known and widely used oil finish blend is called *Tru-Oil* (Gun Stock Finish). It dries fairly hard (for an oil finish) and can be built up to a film on the wood surface. Tru-Oil is available online from Birchwood-Casey (www.birchwoodcasey.com), and Luthiers Mercantile International, Inc. (www.lmii.com).

- **Polyurethane**—I still have to list polyurethane as a musical instrument finish; I know that there are woodworkers out there who are used to using this finish all the time, and can't get past the fact that it is *acoustically* not the best finish. Polyurethane is quite durable, however. If you want to use it, I would try to keep the coats as thin as possible, and as few as possible. And as I have mentioned before, if this is your first and only bowed psaltery, you probably won't know the difference anyway. It will be the best (and only) bowed psaltery finish that you've ever used! Polyurethane is widely available at just about any hardware, woodworking, or general store. Some of the most commonly used brands are Minwax, Cabot, McCloskey, and General Finishes, which are simply brushed or wiped on and allowed to dry.

Finishing Tips:

Finishing is fairly straightforward. Follow the instructions from the manufacturer closely, and don't cut corners. Patience, I believe, is the key to a good finish. Beyond that, here are a few tidbits of advice that I can offer:

- Try to avoid getting drips into the soundhole. Depending on what type of soundhole you've used, you can either: get creative with masking tape, stuff a rag inside the instrument, or just be very careful.

- Don't rush things along or try to handle the instrument before the finish is dry. Even when a finish feels dry to the touch, you can easily leave fingerprint indents in the finish if you pick up the psaltery and hold it for more than a few seconds. Wait a little longer between each step than the manufacturer suggests to ensure that everything is cured, otherwise it may cost you a lot more time down the road.

- Pay attention to detail. I would say that traditionally, hardly anything has been more meticulously finished than musical instruments. Even on furniture, typically only the table *top* is given special attention, with the rest of the body being finished one step lower than the top. Treat the entire instrument as a tabletop! Everything will be seen and held up close.

For a progress update on the bowed psaltery that was built as the project for this book, the pores in the Kwila have been filled with a pore-filler, giving the wood a smooth, glassy surface for the finish to sit on. Then, several coats of shellac were applied and rubbed out to an even, glossy finish.

Front and back views of the psaltery after pore-filling and sanding

The same psaltery after a coat of shellac has been applied — the wood comes alive!

To me, applying the first coat of finish is probably one of the most satisfying parts of the entire building process. The wood just leaps to life with color and vibrancy. Notice how much more pronounced the curls in the redwood become under the shellac. Also, this is my first experience using Kwila, but the back and sides look beautiful. The color and grain texture remind me of graham crackers.

The Bridge

We are getting very close to being able to call our project a musical instrument. With the finishing step out of the way, all that stands between us and musical strings is a small little piece of wood called *the bridge*.

The bridge's function is to transfer all of the strings' vibrations to the soundboard—and from there to the rest of the psaltery. All 25 of the strings will be in direct contact with the bridge. Actually, I shouldn't say *direct*, there is one more piece—the bridge *saddle* that sits atop the bridge—which prevents the strings from gouging too far into the wood. (If the strings were to become embedded too deep into the wood of the bridge, it would greatly inhibit the strings' vibrations and sustain.)

Take a look at the drawing of the bridge:

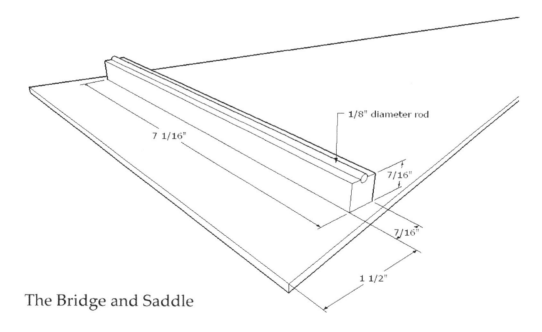

The Bridge and Saddle

The bridge is a simple piece of wood topped with a saddle to protect it from the strings

The length of the bridge will vary, depending on the exact width of your instrument. In any case, when placed 1½" from the bottom of the psaltery, (just in front of the pinblock), the bridge should extend out to about ¼" away from the edge of the psaltery on both sides. I also cut the ends of the bridge off at 80° to match the angle on the sides of the psaltery, along with rounding off the edges lengthwise to give it a bit more of a rounded look overall.

Also, you can apply a finish to the bridge in the same way you've finished the rest of the instrument, or you can leave it unfinished. I like to finish the bridge so it matches the body of the psaltery, and because I believe it helps keep the wood more stable when encountering humidity changes. Also keep in mind that wood gains and looses moisture much faster through the end grain—which will be exposed on the bridge. Apply a few extra coats of finish to the ends of the bridge to help ensure that this sensitive area will be well-sealed.

As for the wood used, it can be just about anything, though it might be a good idea to keep it the same type of wood as the sides/back—if nothing else than for aesthetics. Accordingly, for this project I've used Kwila for the bridge to match the rest of the psaltery.

In my opinion, the bridge should be strong and stable. Weak or unsupported bridges can stress the soundboard—all of the strings are exerting their pressure on the thin softwood top. (Bridge placement will be discussed later.) Without strong reinforcement from the bridge and frame, the soundboard may eventually crack under the immense pressure. (Depending on the number and gauge of strings, bowed psalteries can carry up to 1000 lbs. of pressure or more across all of the strings—though only a fraction of this pressure is directly absorbed by the bridge.)

One additional side-note regarding bridges and the integrity of the soundboard: the higher the bridge, the more downward pressure will be exerted on the soundboard. A very high (tall) bridge can place a great deal of stress on the top, while a low bridge can help alleviate pressure—which can be especially useful for weaker top-woods like Cedar. The ⁷⁄₁₆" tall bridge in the plans, (with another ¹⁄₁₆" of height coming from the upper-half of the ⅛" diameter saddle, making an overall height of ½"), is a fairly conservative height, and probably can't be reduced much more than another ⅛" at most.

The Bridge Saddle:

Traditionally, saddles have been made of a solid metal rod—usually ⅛" in diameter. (And that's exactly what our plan calls for as well.) A lot of builders use brass saddles, but I prefer aluminum. I think it matches the hardware (pins and strings) better, and has a much lower density too. Some prefer using a black plastic rod made of Acetal, though it's frequently sold under DuPont's trade-name: Delrin.

The way I see it, the bridge saddle needs to be *just* strong enough to protect the bridge, but not so dense that it inhibits the strings' vibrations. I put the saddle in the same category as the soundboard: its job is to *pass* the strings vibrations, not *hold* them. Accordingly, a lighter saddle will typically provide the least amount of impedance. However, using a denser bridge saddle will also prolong the sustain of the strings, which may be good or bad depending on how much sustain you want.

Most saddle materials, like brass or aluminum, can be found at your local hardware store. (Aluminum welding rods in ⅛" diameter also work well: just soak and strip off the coating in water.) Another great source is online at McMaster-Carr (www.mcmaster.com). They carry all types of metal and plastic rods—along with just about everything else under the sun.

It should be noted that *density* does not always mean *hardness*. Lead is very dense, but not very hard. To me, the ideal bridge saddle would be one that is exceptionally hard and resistant to the strings' abrasions, and yet very light.

But just out of curiosity, I measured the density of a few rods I had lying around my shop, and listed the results in a table on the next page. Also, a more exhaustive listing of material densities, from wood and metal to plastics and composites, can be found in the appendix section on page 120.

Material	Density (measured at ⅛" diameter)
Brass	1.7 grams/inch
Stainless Steel	1.57 grams/inch
Aluminum	.5 grams/inch
Nylon*	.25 grams/inch
*Type 6/6 Nylon. I also measured a ³⁄₁₆" diameter Acetal rod and got density readings close to Nylon.	

Now, once you have the saddle ready, (you can cut it to length with a hacksaw or a rotary tool with a cutoff wheel), it's time to make a slot in the top of the bridge so the saddle doesn't just roll off the top.

Cutting the Slot for the Saddle:

The slot may be made in any number of ways, some easier or faster than others. All that's needed is to make a ⅛" wide slot approximately ¹⁄₁₆" deep along the length of the top center of the bridge—assuming you are using a saddle with a ⅛" diameter.

Once the slot is cut, there is really no need to glue the saddle into the bridge, as the pressure from the strings does more than enough to hold it down. (Additionally, if you ever re-string your psaltery, and if the saddle is not glued down, it's easy to just turn the saddle around 180° and expose a fresh edge to the strings.)

If you are "power-tool challenged" you could use a file or handsaw to make an indent in the top of the bridge. Such means may not be pretty, but as long as it holds the saddle in place, it's functional. Otherwise, you could again use a dremel and perhaps a cut-off wheel, (and a steady hand!) to carve an indent.

Also, recognizing that most table saw blades have about a ⅛" kerf, you could set the blade on your table saw to cut ⅟₁₆" deep. I have only done this a few times, and I have found that it is much safer (and easier) to leave the bridge *uncut* in a larger piece of wood, and machine the groove first. You can then cut the bridge out afterwards around the indent that you initially made. (Remember: *safety first.*)

Lastly, you could use a table-mounted router. This is the method that I now use, and I find it the fastest and easiest—if you have the proper tools. See the picture of how I routed the Kwila saddle slot below:

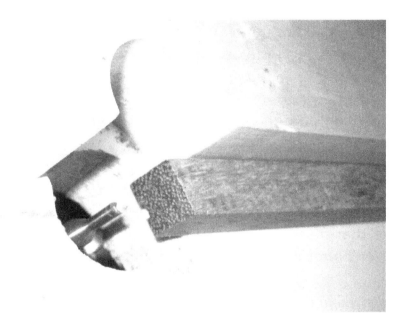

A ⅛" straight-cut router bit is used to make the slot for the bridge saddle

I made a few test cuts on a piece of scrap of identical size to make sure it would be centered on the bridge, and then I just zipped it through the router. The router table setup shown above was just made in my shop from melamine/MDF for the top, 2x4s for the frame, and some scrap wood, bolts and wingnuts for the sliding fence. Conversely, pre-fabricated router tables are commonly available from hardware and woodworking stores.

Bridge Placement:

Now that we have the bridge and saddle all ready to go, we are finally ready to make a musical instrument. We are now ready to put the strings on; but before we do that, we need to do one last critical thing: place the bridge on the soundboard.

Why is this critical?—because the bridge location determines the vibrating lengths of all the strings on the entire psaltery. (Remember when we took great care to measure out the hitch pin holes to the nearest ⅒th of a millimeter?—there was a reason for that.) Again, I should say that it is no big deal if you cannot measure out to exactly a tenth of a millimeter, and as a matter of fact, you are not expected to—but I think it is important to do your best and be as accurate as possible in all phases of construction. The reason for this is a *cumulative effect* on all errors. If you miss by a little here, and again a little there—on each step the errors build up, until finally it becomes so great that some important aspect of the psaltery is affected.

If you have built your bowed psaltery to the specifications of the plan, then the back of the bridge should theoretically be placed exactly 1½" up from the base of the psaltery to give the correct vibrating lengths. However, recognizing that it's not always possible to be dead-on with everything, here's an even better way to determine where to place the bridge:

> *The bridge should be located so that the vibrating length of the shortest string on the right-hand side of the psaltery will be exactly 5¾" long.*

To get an accurate measurement of this, start from the center of the ³⁄₁₆" hitch pin hole, (the one farthest from the tip on the right-hand side of the psaltery), and measure down to the tuning pin hole in the very lower-right corner of the psaltery. Your ruler is now placed along the imaginary line where the first string will run—between the hitch pin and the tuning pin. Now, place the bridge on the soundboard—centered left and right on the soundboard—so that the middle of the bridge saddle will be at 5¾" from the hitch pin. (See the drawing on the following page.)

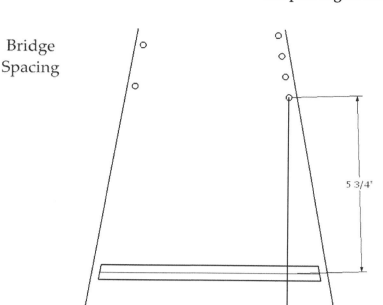

Bridge location is critical to have all the strings sound their best

If your psaltery is slightly too long:

No big deal, just position the bridge according to the plan above, and there will be a small gap between the bridge and the pinblock under the soundboard. This can actually help the strings transfer their vibrations to the soundboard better. However, without the support of the pinblock adjacent to the bridge, the bridge will be little match for the pressure of the strings, and may bow inward at the middle. If this is the case, it is important that the bridge extends close to the edges of the psaltery so that at least the ends of the bridge can be supported by the sides of the psaltery. You can also try decreasing the overall height of the bridge slightly: even $\frac{1}{16}$" shorter will help.

If your psaltery is slightly too short:

There is only so far that you can move the bridge back until it is covering up the holes for the top row of tuning pins. I would try to leave at least $\frac{3}{8}$" to $\frac{1}{2}$" between the back of the bridge and the top row of tuning pins. Just use your best judgment as to where to place it so that a good compromise is reached. If the higher strings are too short—even by ¼" or less in some cases—they will start to sound scratchy, and in extreme cases, be virtually unplayable. However, most of the middle and lower notes on the psaltery should hardly be affected at all.

Once you've found the exact location where you want the bridge to be, you need to somehow mark where you plan to place it. I don't like to write on the wood finish, so I just use a piece of low-tack masking tape and lay it across the location.

While you technically don't have to glue either the saddle or the bridge down, (the strings' pressure will do that), I sometimes like to put a tiny little drop of glue right in the center of the bridge and tack it down. (I still leave the saddle unglued.) This minimal amount of glue is just enough to keep the bridge from slipping around while I am putting the first few strings on. Otherwise, your carefully measured location may get thrown off by a sliding bridge that you didn't notice had moved until you're all finished. I like to use super glue, (aka CA glue), for this job because it sticks well to most types of wood finishes and dries very quickly.

Stringing

Stringing is when this project goes from a triangular wooden box to a musical instrument. It's also probably the most time consuming part of the whole undertaking—especially if you've never done it before. For your first try, I don't think it would be unreasonable to set aside at least two hours for stringing, possibly more. (It of course gets much easier with practice, but with only one instrument to build, that becomes moot.)

Now, the first thing we need is the material to be used for the strings.

Materials Suitable for Music Wire:

Most bowed psalteries today are strung with plain steel music wire. There is really nothing magical about "music" wire—there are no leprechauns in a little music wire factory producing their enchanted strings. Music wire is simply steel wire—with a high tensile strength—that is produced to tight tolerances and consistent diameters.

Online, a few good sources are Musicmaker's (www.harpkit.com) and Folkcraft (www.folkcraft.com). You will need roughly 50 feet of wire. Not really this much wire is used, but it would be a real drag to run out halfway through. Also, it's nice to have extra wire on hand in case a string breaks, or if you need to replace a string for some reason.

For simplicity's sake, I would just use one single gauge: size .012" diameter wire. Ordinarily I would use about three different string gauges, but on an instrument this small (2 octaves) I feel it unnecessary. If you want to learn more about string gauges, you can read more about it in the appendix section on page 110.

If you didn't do the best job gluing the frame together, and you're worried about the string tension stressing your psaltery, you can step down to .010" diameter wire, which will decrease the overall tension on the instrument. You may not get as much volume or fullness of tone with this gauge, but it would be better than a ruined instrument.

If ordering wire online, I would ask the seller if the wire is coated before ordering. Basically, uncoated steel wire can rust and corrode faster than the coated varieties. (And while a little rust on a string is not necessarily that detrimental to the string's tone, it can still be unsightly and will probably shorten the lifespan of the string.)

Locally, I've found a good source of wire that can be used on a shoestring budget: it's found in a certain type of clothesline. The specific type I'm referring to is made by the Lehigh group, and is braided and coated in green vinyl. It's sold in a plastic bag and is listed as 50 ft. x ⁵⁄₃₂" in size. The model number listed on the front is #955.

Now, as a builder, I had oodles and oodles of music wire lying around for this project. But, what fun would that be!? So, in the spirit of a *simple* psaltery, I've chosen to use the above-mentioned clothesline on our project bowed psaltery. Partly for the adventure, and partly to prove that it is a viable option, (though mildly annoying). You have to strip the vinyl coating off, revealing five twisted pairs of steel wire. You then have to untwist these wire pairs to (finally!) get to some useable "music" wire.

Green vinyl-coated clothesline was stripped and used as the strings for our psaltery

Now, in all honesty, in order to build a bowed psaltery, you will probably have to order at least one or two things online anyway—a tuning wrench and 50 zither pins—so I would recommend adding actual music wire onto your order. (For one instrument, it is moderately priced.) But, if you ever find yourself in a jam, and need some wire locally, it may be closer than you think.

On the upside, one clothesline package contains enough wire to string many bowed psalteries, and the inner wires are .012" diameter: exactly the size music wire I would recommend for this psaltery anyway. Also, the wire has a yellow coating on it, which I suspect might be zinc—so it may very well have decent corrosion resistance too.

Now, as long as we are on the topic of makeshift music wire, let me address one last question: how about fishing line? In a nutshell, it can work—how *well* will depend on several factors: the key is getting enough tension on the string. For reference, the .012" steel music wire I mentioned above has a breaking point of nearly 40 pounds. In order to get sufficient tension with a monofilament (nylon) fishing line, I would recommend trying to approach *at least* half this number. Basically, you will need a line much thicker than the steel wire in order to make up for the decreased tensile strength of nylon. (Consider looking at sizes of around .032" diameter nylon.)

Additionally, even if you do find nylon of the correct gauge and tension, nylon is much weaker in terms of abrasion resistance, and I've found that it is susceptible to being cut and sliced through from the sharp bends in the hitch pin's hole.

Regardless of all this, you are certainly free to experiment. With little tension on the strings, you may get decreased volume because so little of the strings' vibrations are being transferred to the soundboard. (Which may be an upside—you won't wake the neighbors!) Tension helps drive the vibrations into the rest of the instrument's body—among other things.

After all this, I trust you have found the right string/wire for your psaltery, now it's time to get down to business!

Inserting the Pins:

I should add a brief disclaimer here: there are many ways to string a bowed psaltery: some are perhaps better than others. What I describe here is simply my own method. You are free to modify, tweak, or otherwise change anything you read here, so long as the end result comes out the way we want: with the strings on the bowed psaltery and making music!

For my method, I find it fastest and easiest to put all the pins into their respective holes first, and then string it afterward. Some builders add one pin at a time. Do whatever suits you best. I will describe my method: so, we begin by driving in all the tuning pins, and then the hitch pins too.

An old tuning wrench was modified into a tuning pin driver for use in a cordless drill

I used the tool pictured above to quickly drive the hitch pins into their holes. (A T-handled wrench was stripped of the handle and ground down to have a few flat faces on the shaft for the chuck to grip.) Using a power tool to drive the pins in is fast—so fast, in fact, that it can burn the wood, which can be bad. (The burnt wood is not as good at holding the thread-paths of the pins.) Because of this, I only use a power drill to drive the hitch pins, not the tuning pins. The hitch pins are stationary, and once they're in, the threads aren't used anyway. But some builders will actually drive the hitch pins in with a hammer. (Not wanting to accidentally crack my fine instrument open like a coconut, I avoid this ape technique.) Do whatever you're comfortable with.

As it has been mentioned earlier, you will need a total of 50 pins. (25 will be used as hitch pins, and 25 will be used as tuning pins.) They go by a lot of names: zither pins, harpsichord pins, tuning pins, autoharp pins, dulcimer pins, etc.—whatever they call them, make sure they are the type that are meant for a ³⁄₁₆" hole, and that they have a hole in the side of them. (I would also recommend using nickel-plated pins as well, if for nothing else than aesthetics, in addition to corrosion resistance.)

I intentionally chose 50 pins for this project, (and therefore 25 strings), because a lot of places will sell the pins in pre-measured quantities of 50. Tuning pins can be bought online from such sites as Elderly, Musicmaker's, and Folkcraft—and while you're at it, pick up a tuning wrench to fit the pins too:

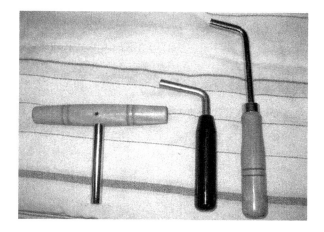

From left to right: T-Handle, L-Handle, and Gooseneck tuning wrenches

Of the three wrenches pictured above, my favorite for *building* is the T-Handle. It lets you get better downward pressure when driving the pins, and is easy to turn with one hand. On the other hand, my favorite for *tuning* is the gooseneck wrench on the far right. Actually, any of these will do, it's just that certain wrenches make certain jobs easier to perform.

Next, carefully drive all the tuning pins into their holes at the base of the psaltery; orient them so that all of the holes in the pins are facing toward the front of the psaltery. (Actually, I *do* use a cordless drill to start the tuning pins into their holes: I drive the pins easily through the soundboard and feel an abrupt increase in resistance when I hit the hard maple pinblock—which is when I know to stop using the drill and drive them in the rest of the way by hand.)

If you've drilled angled tuning pin holes, take extra care to make sure you start the pins at the correct angle. Again, some builders will drive these pins in with a hammer; I chose not to.

As for the depth of the tuning pins, leave them a good ways out of their holes to allow extra room for winding the string onto the pin. The idea is that once you have wound the string around the tuning pin about 3–4 times, it should be as deep into the pinblock as possible, (to maximize the surface area of the threads contacting the pinblock), but not *too* deep.

By *too* deep I mean that the string starts to scrape and abrade the top of the psaltery as it's forced into the soundboard. This is not only bad for the soundboard, but since the pin can't really go any deeper, it may also strip out the threads in the pinblock—greatly decreasing its tuning stability and longevity. Since it's worse to go too deep than too shallow, I tend to leave myself a little bit of breathing room in this area.

It may take a few trial-and-error tests to get the height correct. One thing though—for aesthetics' sake—make sure that all the tuning pins are at roughly the same height.

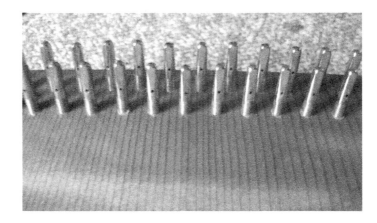

An overall look at the tuning pins before the strings are wound on them

Once we have all the tuning pins inserted, next up are the hitch pins. When you insert the hitch pins, orient them so that the hole runs toward the tuning pins. Make an imaginary line going from the hitch pin to the corresponding tuning pin. Just go right down the line and align each hitch pin ahead of time.

Now, in terms of the depth to drive each hitch pin, I like to go just about as low as the pin will allow—with a little bit of working room of course. (Remember that you still have to thread the string through the pin's hole.) I recommend making a concerted effort to try and drive all the pins to one uniform height. This makes playing easier, and generally looks better too. Some builders prefer to sink the pins just deep enough so that the threads aren't showing. You can see how deep I like mine in the picture below:

A close-up shot of some hitch pins, giving an approximate idea of their depth

Notching the Hitch Pins:

Now comes time to notch the hitch pins—actually, a lot of builder's notch their hitch pins *before* they insert them into the psaltery. The reason I prefer to notch them while they're in the psaltery is because it's incredibly easy: the psaltery is already holding all the pins upright for you.

Basically, what we will be doing is putting a shallow groove in the corner of the pin, in the back center. This groove is for the string to come up and over the top of the pin, and rest in. Without it, the string would slide off the top of the hitch pin when we bring it up to tension.

To the left is a picture of a hitch pin that shows the path of the string, and illustrates what we are trying to accomplish. Note that you must take care to ensure that the holes through the hitch pins are all facing the same direction—running parallel with the length of the psaltery—otherwise you'll be notching the wrong side of the pin.

The slow way to do this is with a hand file: taking a triangular file and carefully filing a notch in each pin. But I prefer using a rotary tool (i.e., Dremel, etc.) with a thin cut-off wheel to just run a smooth curve into the upper back of each pin. I leave all the pins in the psaltery, and just buzz away. The entire process probably takes two or three minutes to do all the pins. Once done, I take a brush and gently brush away the metal dust that has accumulated on the soundboard; a can of compressed air does wonders too. You may have to turn some of the hitch pins about an eighth of a turn outward to get a better angle and clearance with the tool.

Once we have notched all the hitch pins, and have them all facing the right way, we're ready to actually put the strings on.

Preparing for Stringing:

This is where things can get a little tricky. My first piece of advice to you—in order to prevent a lot of fumblings and bumblings—is to clamp your psaltery down to a table or workbench. Obviously, you don't want to ruin the finish on your instrument, so you have to use care when clamping.

Notice in the picture to the left that the clamp is actually pressing down harmlessly on two or three hitch pins—*not* on the wood. Also, the instrument itself is resting on a pad of carpet, so the finish on the bottom won't be scratched either. I've found that the best type of clamp for this job is a one-handed bar-clamp, which usually has large plastic guards to keep from marring the clamped material. These types of clamps are available both online and at most hardware stores.

Now, the basic idea here is to first tie the string onto the hitch pin, and then run it over the bridge and into the hole of the corresponding tuning pin. Then, you wind the string onto the tuning pin by rotating the pin clockwise until the string is reasonably taut. But, before we jump right in, it will help to be prepared, so I recommend grabbing a few tools.

First, get a nice pair of wire cutters. Actually, for only one psaltery, you don't need a *nice* pair—but cheaper ones tend to wear out much faster, especially considering the hardness of this tough music wire. I use a pair of cutters with carbide-tipped jaws meant to be used in orthodontics to cut the wires for braces! They look almost the same as the day I got them: nice and sharp—I can't say the same for the softer steel that was used in some of my cheaper cutters.

Second, get a pair of needle-nose pliers. This is used to put a bend in the end of the wire to keep it from slipping out at the tuning pin, (more on this later in the chapter).

Third, I recommend using a pair of vise-grip pliers to help pull the knots tight on the hitch pin. You could use a pair of regular pliers, but I find vise-grips—sometimes referred to as locking pliers—are much easier and safer to use. (This is because you don't have to squeeze when you are pulling on the line—they lock down onto the wire.) They allow you to use all your strength on pulling, and virtually eliminate the chance of slipping.

Last of all, (besides your tuning wrench, of course), I like to use a digital tuner while stringing. I figure: you've got your hands on the string right here, and the wrench is already on the tuning pin—why not bring the string all the way up to tune right off the bat? (For more details on tuning, see the chapter on tuning on page 69.)

Bringing a string up to full tune right away also helps prevent problems with slipping wire. For instance, you may find that three winds around the tuning pin aren't enough to hold the string at full tension, and you may have to wind more rotations of string onto the pin. You won't know how many rotations are enough to hold the wire until you actually bring it all the way up to playing tension.

Once we have all the tools and materials gathered, and our psaltery is clamped down, we are ready to begin with the first step of stringing.

Tying the String to the Hitch Pin:

This is fairly straightforward: take a length of string, and thread it through the hole of the hitch pin for the shortest string. Start from the side of the pin facing the tip of the psaltery and thread about six inches of wire in toward the bridge. Next, wrap one rotation around the pin and bring it back out through the hole, back towards the tip of the psaltery, with a few inches of excess sticking out. (This excess is left to easily grab and pull tight with the vise-grips later on.)

Now, depending on the wire you used, and the size of the hole in your pins, one rotation should be enough to hold the full tension of the string without coming out—but not always. If you happened to use very thin music wire, and/or the hole in your pin is larger than usual, you may need two rotations. I use and illustrate just one rotation for this book.

Notice that it doesn't need to be particularly tight—yet. We will pull it tight and bring everything up to tension once the string is wound onto the tuning pin.

Wire is loosely tied to the hitch pin, with the long end going down to the tuning pin

This process is for one string. Only tie and wind one string at a time. I recommend stringing the two shortest strings—one on the left, and one on the right—first. The tension of these two strings should then hold the bridge and saddle steady, and you can proceed right down the line, from the lower right section, up toward the tip, and then back down the left side of the psaltery.

Winding the String onto the Tuning Pin:
This is the hard part; at least, to do it well, it takes practice.

Take the long end of the string that you've just tied to the hitch pin, and put it in the groove you made in the hitch pin, and bring it over the bridge and through the hole of the tuning pin. Pull the string somewhat taut and measure out about 2" beyond the tuning pin, (about three finger-widths), and cut the wire off. This distance will vary depending on a lot of factors, but typically 2" should be enough for about three to four winds around the tuning pin, which should be an adequate amount to hold the fully tuned tension of the string. If you find that the string is slipping when brought up to full tension, you will need more windings: this is done by increasing the length of string wound onto the tuning pin end. I used roughly 2" on this project, and it was enough to hold all the strings under tension.

Next, take the needle-nose pliers and bend a sharp downward 90° crook into the wire. I make this hook about ⅛" up from the end of the wire. This will prevent the wire from slipping out of the pin's hole while you are winding it. Here's a picture of approximately what you should now have on the tuning pin side:

A sharp bend is put in the wire to prevent it from slipping out of the tuning pin hole

One other thing to notice in the above picture: look at the other tuning pins: see how neatly and tightly wound the strings are spooled onto the tuning pins? It is hard to do this on your first try, but try to be as neat as possible. This is where drilling the tuning pin holes at an angle will really help you keep things tidy. Beyond just looking better, winding the string neatly onto the pin also ensures that the string will not start riding up on the pin; if the string were to start coiling *up* on the tuning pin, (rather than down), it could eventually make it very difficult to fit a tuning wrench over the pin's head.

Now, make sure that the string is sitting in the hitch pin's groove, and pull the wire taut. (If you pull too hard, you will un-bend the crook you put in the end of the wire, so take care.) While you have the string taut, begin with the other hand to use the tuning wrench and wind the tuning pin down into its hole; while you do this, pay attention to where the wire is wrapping itself onto the tuning pin. You want the string to start winding just below the hole and have tightly compacted rows of wire forming just below it.

Keeping the wire taut at all times is the key to controlling where and how it winds onto the tuning pin. All the while, of course, you have to make sure that the string is still sitting in the hitch pin's groove—it can easily and frequently fall off. This is where you will realize why I recommended clamping the psaltery down, otherwise it could take an octopus to do all these jobs.

Continue winding the string until it is taut and firmly resting against the bridge saddle. Take care on your "landing" when the string gets tight enough to make first contact with the bridge saddle. Once the string is fully tightened, it becomes much harder to move the string to the left or right along the saddle. The string should be tight enough to be able to pluck, and you should hear a nice *ping* sound from the string. Not too tight though, save that for tuning. (Or you can tune it immediately after it's wound onto the pin.) If you do happen to break the string, back the tuning pin out to its original height and start over.

And, that's all there is to it! *Rinse and repeat.* But there are a few loose ends we still need to still clear up:

Final Touches:

Once you have the first string wound onto the tuning pin, don't bother trying to tune it up to full tension—it will just slip at the knot you tied at the hitch pin. What we need to do is pull the excess wire as tight as possible and trim it back.

This step seems pretty straightforward, but just be careful, and always pull slightly up and away from the psaltery. Otherwise, if you do happen to slip, well, I can't imagine that it would be an enjoyable experience—for you or the psaltery.

Please note: avoid using the pliers on any part of the string that will be left on the instrument, especially in the area where it will be bowed. A pair of pliers can very easily put a permanent kink in music wire—even after it has been brought up to full tension.

A pair of vise-grip pliers is used to safely pull the knot tight

Doing a good job of tightening the knots will decrease the psaltery's break-in time because there will be less "settling" that needs to occur with the string. Otherwise, if you bring the string up to tune with loose knots, it will go out of tune because the vibrations shake the slack out of the knot—reducing the overall tension (and pitch) of the string.

Next, we need to trim off the excess wire. I like to get as close to the hitch pin as possible. If you leave a length of wire, (especially plain-steel wire), hanging out the pin's hole, it can possibly prick you when you are playing.

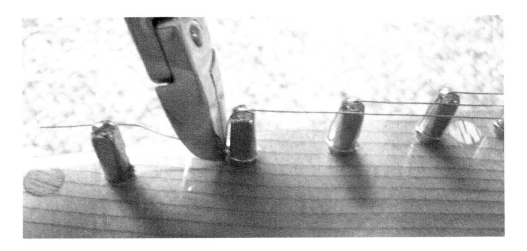

A pair of wire cutters is used to cut the wire off right at the edge of the pin

In order to get very close to the excess wire, you need to make the cut with the very tip of the pliers. The pliers' jaws are quickly fatigued and dulled when cutting with the tip, so make every cut count! Once you're done, run your finger over the edge of the pin several times to make sure that you've cut the wire back far enough and that there is no risk of a cut or poke.

Tuning

First thing's first: let's establish just what exactly the range of this instrument really is, and what pitch each string will be tuned to:

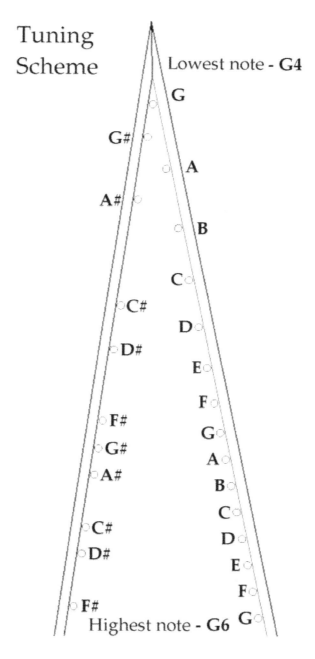

In terms of which *octave* all of these notes are found on, refer to a piano keyboard. The lowest note is the first G above middle C. (Also notated as G4.)

Playing range for this bowed psaltery (G4 to G6)

Now that you know what pitch to tune all the strings to, all you need is a reference point. If you have a piano or keyboard, you can use that. Also, if you are on a shoestring budget, and you are just getting your feet wet in musical instruments, I've found a decent online tuning program at:

http://www1.ocn.ne.jp/~tuner/tuner_e.html

(This is a Japanese site, and the program was originally meant to tune a Japanese instrument called a "shakuhachi.")

Otherwise, if you plan on playing your psaltery with any regularity, or if you are going to travel at all with it, I suggest taking a look at a digital tuner.

Digital Tuners:

Way back when I tried to tune my very first bowed psaltery by ear with a keyboard—after a few minutes of vain attempts—I decided that there had to be a better way to tune my bowed psaltery. Let me show you an easy, accurate, and inexpensive solution:

Not sure if a string is in tune? A digital tuner tells you exactly what note's being played

Pictured on the opposite page is a handy little gadget that I don't think I'd be able to live without. This small little handheld digital tuner has a built-in microphone that "hears" the note you're playing, and shows you whether it's sharp, flat, or in tune. In the picture, you can see that the note is G, and that it's perfectly in tune because the green light in the middle is lit up. Had the note been out of tune, the flat (b) or sharp (#) light would be lit up and the swing-arm needle would be pointing to the left or right.

One of the best places to pick up one of these tuners is on eBay, or on Amazon.com. Otherwise, if you need one quickly, chances are some music shops will stock them in your local area for a bit more. I picked up my first one locally from Groth music.

There are all sorts of tuners, but you have to make sure that you get one that is *chromatic*—that is to say, one that will pick up and tune any notes, including flats and sharps. Some will only do certain strings, such as a tuner meant specifically for a guitar. One that was highly recommended to me for both reliability and economy was the Korg CA-30; you should be able to find one for around $20. This is the tuner that I use, and I've been completely satisfied with its performance.

You may also notice in some photos that I use a contact microphone attached to my tuner; I added this to make it easier to tune, which I clip directly to the bridge or to one of the tuning pins. It basically substitutes the open-air microphone that is built into the CA-30 for a soft alligator clip that physically senses the strings' vibrations. Doing this allows me to pluck the string even very lightly and still get a good reading on the pitch. Otherwise, you have to either bow the string or pluck it loudly with your fingernail. (The actual intended purpose for the contact microphone is to allow a person to tune their instrument in a noisy environment where the built-in mic may get confused.)

The model number for the contact mic for the Korg CA-30 tuner is: CM-100. Again, this mic is available from the usual online places: eBay, and Amazon.com. (You might have trouble finding this item locally.)

Tuning a String for the First Time:

If you're tuning your instrument for the very first time after stringing it, your procedure will be a little bit different than an everyday tuning.

For one, now that you have strung the psaltery, it begins a break-in process. During this time, the strings settle into their spots and the instrument as a whole adjusts to the added tension. In subtle movements, the frame of the psaltery will flex and react to the hundreds of pounds of pressure that is now pulling on it.

Overall, your psaltery's strings will tend to go flat—that is to say, the tension will be reduced and the pitch will be lower. Within a week or two most fluctuations should subside. But in order to speed this process along, certain adjustments can be made to help the psaltery settle in faster.

As I briefly explained at the end of the stringing chapter, the better a job you do when tightening the knots at the hitch pin, the shorter the break-in period will be. This is because when you bring a string up to tune and subsequently play it with the bow, the vibrations of the string will tend to shake the slack out of the line, causing the string's tension to drop. As a matter of fact, when you first tune it, chances are that by the time you get to the last string, the first string will probably already be out of tune!

Don't be discouraged by this immediate loss of tension—it's a normal process with every new bowed psaltery. This is why the first time tuning will be different than your everyday tuning. Do you think that we should try and get the string to an absolutely perfect pitch knowing that it will probably be out of tune by the time we get to the last string? *No, don't worry about it!*

For our first tuning, it will be sloppy. Don't worry about getting things dead-on. You won't really be playing it after the first tuning anyway. You're just looking to bring it up to the correct note, but it doesn't have to be perfect. First tune it sloppily applying the techniques for first tuning that I'll describe below, and then afterward retune it according to the everyday tuning section. (See *everyday tuning* in the next section for the basic mechanics of tuning.) The psaltery will get more and more stable with each tuning.

So what can we do to help settle the psaltery in faster? Here are some tips:

- For the first time, tune the string a little bit sharp (high); a half-step should be enough. If it is G, bring it up to G#, and so forth. (Though, take care not to go too far beyond the string's intended pitch, otherwise it may break.)

- Once you have brought the string up a little sharp, "balance" the string by taking your finger and pressing down on the string (somewhat) firmly to help settle it in. Chances are that the pitch will immediately go down below where it should be—even if you had tuned it sharp.

- Retune the note sharp again—perhaps a little less this time—and repeat this process a few more times until it seems as if the string is starting to stabilize. But just don't press *too* hard.

- Try pressing down on the string in different areas to settle in different areas—in the middle, near the hitch pin, and near the bridge.

- Even if it seems as if the string has become perfectly stable, tune it ever so slightly sharp, never slightly flat. In this beginning phase, the strings almost always loosen and go flat, and not sharp. Chances are, the frame, soundboard, and bridge will all flex and react to the new tension, though usually imperceptibly to the eye.

On our demonstration psaltery, it had pretty stable tuning very quickly. After the second tuning, nearly all the strings were still in tune after playing some songs. By the next day, only two or three strings were flat, but not by much.

Now that you have seen how to help accelerate the stabilization phase, it's time to learn just how to tune the psaltery for playing.

Everyday Tuning:

Unlike the first time we tune the psaltery, everyday tuning will be times when we want to get the strings exactly in tune for playing. In most cases, they should already be very close to in tune, so very few coarse adjustments should be necessary.

Because of the finer adjustments that are involved, I like to use a long gooseneck tuning wrench for everyday tuning because you can get a lot more leverage than the shorter L or T handle wrenches. (See tuning wrench photo on page 59.) More leverage also equates to being able to make more minute adjustments, which is helpful for the shortest and highest strings. (However, a gooseneck wrench is not required. If I had to pick only one wrench to own for both building and tuning, I think it would be the T-handle wrench.)

To raise the pitch of a given string, turn the wrench clockwise; to lower the pitch, turn the wrench counter-clockwise. Turn the wrench slowly and in a controlled manner. *It's strongly recommended to either pluck or bow the string while you are tightening it.* Not only is this necessary to hear if the string is coming into tune, but more importantly, it will prevent you from accidentally tightening the wrong string.

When you turn the wrench, you should be able to audibly hear the pitch change up or down on the string, depending on which way you are turning the wrench. If you don't hear any change in pitch when you turn the wrench, *stop immediately:* trace the string you are trying to tune: start from the hitch pin and go back down to the corresponding tuning pin and make sure that that pin matches the one that you are turning with the wrench. If you continue to tighten the wrong pin, the string will break.

The order that the strings are tuned in makes no difference; whatever is fastest and most convenient for you. For your first time, I would suggest starting with the lowest note at the tip and proceeding down to the base of the psaltery on the right-hand side, and then work from the tip to the base on the left side. The lowest notes are the easiest to tune.

Here are a few more tuning tips:

- On the tuning chart, I have written the notes on the left-hand side all in sharps (#) for clarity. A-sharp is the same note as B-flat, and D-sharp is the same as E-flat, and so on. It is akin to seeing the glass half empty or half full.

- It is much more common for strings to be just slightly too low (flat) than to be sharp. The pins have a tendency to slowly unwind, not tighten. (Unless there is a rise in humidity, in which case the wood and strings can be stretched.)

- Whenever possible, try to tune a string *up* to a given pitch, rather than go too far and have to bring the pitch back *downward*. (This of course excludes the first time you tune a newly built psaltery.) If you tune a string down to the right pitch, the section of the string running from the bridge to the tuning pin may be slightly looser than the section of string running from the bridge to the hitch pin. Lightly balancing the string (as discussed on page 73) may help remedy this.

Tuning is usually quick and easy and should become a regular part of caring for your bowed psaltery. With a little practice, it shouldn't take more than a few minutes. Also, depending on how often you play, you may not have to retune your instrument very often; or it may just need a very tiny tweaking. When I named this section "everyday tuning," I didn't necessarily mean that you'd have to tune it *every* day.

Before we can play this instrument as it was intended, we need a bow. (You can pluck away at it though, which is fun too.) But let's take a look at the options for a bow in the next chapter.

The Bow

Fiddlesticks, what to use for a bow? Up until this point, all we've made is a *plucked* psaltery; but we want to be able to *bow* it in order to bring out the full potential of this instrument's amazing sound. There are a few bow choices available for those who play the bowed psaltery, but unlike the violin, there is certainly no standardized shape or size.

When compared to bows for other bowed instruments, a psaltery's bow is typically smaller and lighter: mainly because the playing style is much different than a violin, cello, etc. On a bowed psaltery, there is much more up and down movement required, rather than the lateral strokes seen on a violin. Because you must be continually moving the bow up and down the length of the psaltery, (also requiring you to extend your arm out farther), a much shorter and lighter bow is used for more agility. More details on this can be found in the chapter on playing on page 87.

Basically, all the bows used fall into two categories: store-bought violin bows, and homemade bows. Both are capable of bringing out the beautiful and haunting sound of the bowed psaltery; which type of bow to use will boil down to your needs and personal preference. I'll discuss both options below.

Fractional sized violin bows:

Fractional sized violin bows are basically bows that were meant to be played on a violin, but are used on a bowed psaltery. A standard violin is called a ¼ size violin, and accordingly, a full size violin bow is referred to as a ¼ bow. Most find this full-sized bow, at nearly 30 inches in length, to be far too cumbersome and heavy to use on a bowed psaltery. Instead, what can be used instead is a bow meant for a fractional sized violin.

There are several sizes of fractional violin bows, ranging from ¾ down to ¹⁄₁₆. (These fractional sizes are not literal: that is, a ¼ violin bow is not one fourth the size of a ¼ bow.) They all have the same sized frog at the end, but each bow gets progressively shorter. I've also noticed a little bit of variation between bow lengths, even among those that are supposed to be the same size.

Here's a brief table estimating the standard sizes and what I have actually encountered:

Bow Size	Bow Length
4/4	~ 29 to 30 inches
3/4	~ 27 inches
1/2	~ 24 to 25 inches
1/4	~ 21 to 22 inches
1/8	~ 19 to 20 inches
1/16	~ 17 to 18 inches

Personally, I use a 1/16 size violin bow. Some people like the bow to be slightly longer, going up to a 1/8 or 1/4 size bow. In special cases, even larger sizes are used when very long notes need to be played.

There are a lot of advantages to using a fractional sized violin bow, and a few disadvantages too. The main advantage is that the violin bow is the result of hundreds of years of refinement in bow making, and in my opinion, gives the best overall sound.

If you are at all interested in learning about bows and how they've changed over the years, I highly recommend tracking down an out-of-print book through your local library, called *"The bow, its history, manufacture, and use"* by Henry Saint-George. (See the bibliography on page 123 for more information.)

The hairs on a violin bow are arranged flat so that a lot more hair makes contact with the string, resulting in a fuller, more even sound. To be honest, in a lot of cases you can barely hear a difference between a violin bow and a homemade bow, but under certain circumstances and on some notes, the extra hairs can reduce the scratchiness of the sound that is sometimes heard. Because of this, it also seems to give more consistent results and can compensate for shortcomings in playing technique.

Think of a homemade bow, with its round cord of hair, as a solo singer, or a duet or trio—only a few hairs are contacting the string, so the sound is more focused, but it's not as full. (This is not necessarily a bad thing.) But, if one of those voices falters somehow, (by hitting the string in the wrong way somehow), it will be quite noticeable. Now, think of a violin bow as a larger chorus of voices—a broader band of hair is contacting the string, so it sounds fuller and more blended. If a few voices falter, you can hardly notice because the other voices are still heard. This is the best way I can describe the sound difference between the two bows, and why I prefer the predictability of a violin bow.

Additionally, a violin bow has an adjustable frog, (the piece that holds the hair at the base of the bow), which allows you to adjust the tension of the hair by turning a knob on the end of the bow. This lets you compensate for playing in different environments and humidity levels, and also prolongs the life of the hair and the bow.

Two big advantages of a violin bow: adjustable hair tension, and a wide band of hair

Now, for the downsides of using a violin bow: primarily, there is the cost. Seeing as how a homemade bow is almost free, violin bows are considerably more expensive! And because of the odd sizes required, it may also be more difficult to find one. However, eBay usually has sellers with smaller bow sizes available for anywhere between $20 and $30 shipped. They are, of course, of all different levels of quality, some I have found to be quite good, and some to be of lower quality.

The second disadvantage is that a violin bow looks a little boring. For period musicians and re-enactments, etc. a violin bow might look a bit too common-place when compared to the archaic-looking homemade bows. I guess I also like to have everything match too—such as having a matching Kwila bow for the Redwood/Kwila bowed psaltery I built for this project.

One last disadvantage, (though rather insignificant), is that due to the width of the violin bow's band of hair, the bow might be unable to get in between the pins on some smaller psalteries. (Obviously the one that we built has the pins spaced far enough apart to allow a violin bow to comfortably pass between the hitch pins.) This is only problematic when the hitch pins have been crammed down to almost ⅜" between pins, which is rare.

For me, the determining factor in choosing a violin bow was based on sound. Because of the orientation of the hairs, (a flat ribbon), I find it gives a full, predictable sound. Now, before you write off making a bow yourself, let's move on to the next section and hear the other side of the case!

Homemade bows:

Chances are, a homemade bow will be entirely sufficient for making music. A lot of it boils down to personal preference and getting used to the bow itself. It's like driving an automatic transmission versus a manual. (Automatic only for me, thank you!) If you play either kind of bow for long enough, you will be able to get good sound out of it, and simply out of habit you may never want to switch to another type of bow.

The main advantage to a homemade bow is cost and simplicity. You can probably make the actual wood part of the bow simply from the scraps leftover from the wood of the psaltery's frame. After that, all you need is some bow hair and you're done. (You will also need some rosin, but this is needed for both types of bows regardless.)

The reason why we don't just make a violin-type bow is that they are rather difficult to make—especially for a first attempt. They require precisely graduating the stick, giving it a camber with an alcohol lamp, along with making the tiny parts for the frog and the angled mortise blocks (usually left unglued to make re-hairing easier) for keeping the hair in place on both ends.

With a homemade bow, we have complete freedom to make the bow in whatever shape we want—within reason, of course. Some people prefer to include a wider end to function as a handle, while others make a completely symmetrical bow that can be held from either end—similar to a traditional style archery bow. In the proceeding plans, I'll leave the final shape up to you, but I'll give some suggestions to help you along.

The main disadvantage, as I seen it, with these homemade bows is that the hair is formed into a round cord and tied off into knots on both ends. Because of how the hair is shaped, not as many hairs contact the string, so the resulting sound can be thinner than a violin bow. An upside to this is that you may be able to jet around a little faster on the strings with a round cord of hair versus a flat ribbon.

The second disadvantage is the fact that the hair of the bow is fixed, and always under tension. While I haven't had any problems because of this yet, it must affect the longevity of the bow. I've noticed in one bow I made several months ago that the tension on the hair is noticeably less than when I first made it. I'm not sure if this is a result of a change in humidity and environment, or if the ends of the wood are slowly being pulled together under the hair's tension; it's nice to be able to adjust the hair to the exact tension that you want.

If this is your first bowed psaltery, I would recommend at least making yourself one or two bows—they're incredibly easy to make. Actually, if you find that you really like playing the bowed psaltery, I'd recommend trying both types of bows: a violin bow and a homemade one, and see which one you like the best.

Making a Bow:

The first step in making your own bow is beginning with a bow blank. The blank is a section of wood that we will use to cut out the pattern of a bow. You can use scraps leftover from the wood of the frame of your psaltery, or any other strong hardwood. For stability's sake, I'd also recommend using wood that is quartersawn, though this is not absolutely essential. (You can read the discussion on quartersawn wood in the appendix on page 105 for more information.) Fortunately, the Kwila that I used for the psaltery and bow were both quartersawn—through no intentional foresight of my own!

Shown below is the size of the blank that I used, which will give you a bow about 16 inches long. You are free to alter the length if you want a bow that is slightly longer or shorter.

Bow Blank

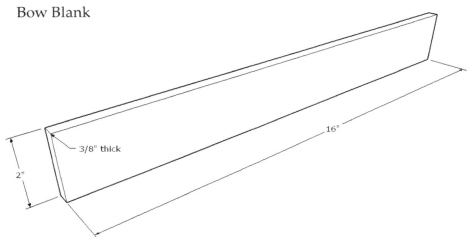

A blank is cut to the overall dimensions of the bow, and then roughed out to shape

Once you've cut the blank to the right dimensions, decide what you want the bow to look like when it's done, and draw the pattern out on the blank. Then, use a bandsaw or scroll saw to remove the majority of the waste from the blank. In the spirit of experimentation, I decided to make a symmetrical bow this time, as I've never tried this shape before.

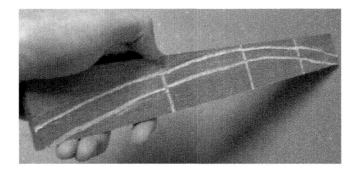

Almost any bow design will work; chose one that suits you best

Once you have the bow in its rough state, you can use various tools to chisel, plane, sand, scrape, rasp, etc. a more refined look to the bow. Sharp 90° angles aren't very comfortable to hold, so try to fit the bow to your hand and make it smooth.

Once the bow is fully shaped and smooth, we have to make a thin cut in each end of the bow to hold the horsehair. I use a bandsaw for this, but any saw with a thin kerf—like a handsaw—will do fine. (I wouldn't use a regular tablesaw blade for this because the blades are usually too thick, and being that the bow is already only ⅜" thick, it won't leave much wood on either side of the slot.)

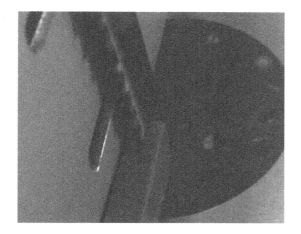 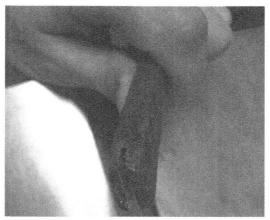

The bow's hair is run through saw-kerf slots cut in the center of the bow on each end

Before you add the hair, this may be a good time to apply a finish to the bow. Otherwise, if you try to do it afterwards, the wood finish might accidentally contaminate the bow hair when you are applying the finish.

Now, for the question of what to use for bow hair—there are two types: real horsehair, and synthetic. For a bow like ours, which has a fixed amount of tension, I would recommend going with synthetic bow hair. The reason for this is because of stability—if we have no way of adjusting the tension, we'll need hair that will be as impervious to environmental changes as possible. Synthetic bow hair is basically plastic, so it shouldn't absorb as much ambient moisture as its organic counterpart. And while some say that real horsehair sounds better, (most violin bows use natural horsehair), I think that to most psaltery players, the difference is slight—I really can't tell the difference at all.

One brand of synthetic bow hair that was recommended to me, (which I have also had good experiences with), is Hervex. It is available online from such sites as Elderly (www.elderly.com), Musicmaker's (www.harpkit.com), and Folkcraft (www.folkcraft.com), and only costs a few dollars for a hank. One hank of horsehair should be able to make two to three psaltery bows. (This just shows you how much less hair is used on our homemade bows versus a real violin bow.)

Once you have the bow and hair all ready, take about half of the hank of hair, (or ⅓ of the hank if you're trying to stretch it into several bows), and tie a knot in one end. Next, hold the hair by the end of the knot so all the hair is dangling down, and comb it with a fine-tooth comb. Get all the tangles out, and get the hair as straight and even as possible.

Next, the bow hair will first be slipped into the first notch on one side of the bow—being held in by the knot—and then stretched over the end and into the other slot. The idea is to tie the hair short enough so that there is still adequate tension once the hair has made it over the hump, but not so short that you practically have to break the bow to get the hair into the slot. It will take a little bit of experimentation to find where to tie off the other end.

The hair is first put in the slot on one end, then stretched into the slot on the other end

One way to tell if you've got the hair tight enough—and straight enough—is that there should be no slack hairs in the bow. If there are slack or loose hairs, take the hair off the end, remove the knot from the one end, re-comb it, and tie it again. It only takes a few seconds to retry; keep at it until you get all the hairs tight. You should have to exert a fair amount of pressure on the bow to get the knot over the last hump. (Though in all honesty, I don't think I could break this bow with my bare hands if I tried my hardest—so, make sure the bow is sound and strong, and then put the hair on tight!)

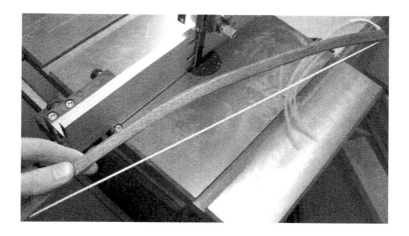

A bow with the hair under tension, with a "pony tail" hanging off the end

Now, once you've got the hair tied off to your liking, you'll have a lot of excess to trim back. You can either leave the knots as they are, and trim the hair back to about ¼" above the knot, or you can try the following trick:

Thin CA glue (super glue) is applied and allowed to wick deep into the knot's core

If you use very thin, water-like consistency CA glue, you can wick the glue all the way to the middle of the hank, and effectively "lock" the knot in place. Once this is done, and the glue is fully cured, you can take a scissors and cut the hair off directly above the knot. (Don't allow any glue to get on the area of the hairs that will be played on the psaltery!)

Rosin up the Bow:

After this cleanup stage, we're all done with the bow! You'll need to get some rosin and apply it to the hair to help it "grab" the strings. Rosin is widely available at almost all music stores, locally and online, for dirt cheap. It comes in a cake and is slid across the bow's hairs back and forth. There are two varieties—light and dark. The dark is slightly softer, and gives a little bit more grab to the string, for a coarser sound. I like to use the dark because I think it helps the bow grab the lower strings better, but I really can hardly tell the difference between the two—either one will work fine.

With a new bow on your first time, it's necessary to prime the bow with rosin. The slick surface of a new rosin cake is not very conducive to filling the hair with rosin. To remedy this, you can roughen the surface of the rosin by cutting criss-crosses in it with a sharp knife. (You could also use coarse sandpaper to achieve similar results.) For the first time, run the rosin up and down the taut bow-hair several times until it seems to be sticky. In newly made bows this may take a minute, but in the future you should only have to give a few quick, occasional passes with the rosin to prepare the bow.

Rosin up the bow, it's time to play!

Playing

I enjoy playing the bowed psaltery and I mainly play simple melodies for personal enjoyment. I'm certainly no musician: I consider myself mostly just a builder—and *appreciator*—of bowed psalteries.

This chapter is meant only to give a very basic and rudimentary overview of playing mechanics. Advanced playing techniques—such as using multiple bows—I'm afraid, are mostly beyond me; I will leave that task to another book, and another musician.

Basic Mechanics:

Maybe you have been looking at pictures of the bowed psaltery, with its *many* strings, and you are wondering exactly how you *play* this peculiar instrument—or *bow* it for that matter! I think you'll be surprised to see that it's much simpler than you may think:

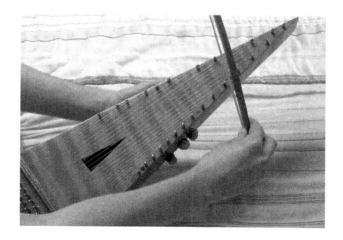

The bowed psaltery is played along the sides of the instrument

The above picture should clear up most of the confusion for anyone who has not yet played a bowed psaltery. The strings are bowed along the *sides* of the instrument, not the *middle*. The bow is run in between the pins on the right and left sides of the instrument, where there is an opening and only one string can be bowed at a time. Sharps and flats are played by reaching over to the left side of the instrument.

In terms of how the instrument is held, there are a variety of positions, with no officially correct one, though certain postures are more common than others.

The most common way practiced is to hold the tip of the psaltery out away from your body with your left hand grasping it about two-thirds the way up. Then, the base of the instrument is nestled either on the inside of your elbow, or against your abdomen. The right hand holds the bow and does all of the playing. A variation on this is to just sit down and set it on your lap, loosely supporting the end with your left hand. Experiment to find which position you are most comfortable with—both in holding and playing the psaltery.

Playing Notes and Scales:

Now with a light grip, run the bow along some of the strings in between the hitch pins. If you've applied enough rosin to the bow, your psaltery should give a nice sound as you run the bow across the strings.

Try to keep the bow moving even after you've let it off the string. This is to ensure that you don't accidentally stop the bow before you lift it off the string. If this happens, the sound of the string will come to an abrupt stop and sound a bit awkward. You are after smooth, fluid arm movements.

Practice moving up and down the right-hand side of the psaltery—playing each note as you go. You may even be able to play a song by ear.

Next, practice reaching over to the left side and angling the bow to play all of the notes on the left-hand side. With a little bit of practice, you should be able to get some nice sounds out of it in a very short time. However, don't be discouraged if you also create some horrendous squeals from the psaltery on your first time. Like anything, it does take some practice, and many mistakes may simply be due to very slight problems in technique.

Anyhow, you may notice when you're playing that some strings seem to sound a little strange or off, sometimes scratchy, or sometimes metallic, and this may be due to several reasons. See if some of these tips don't help:

- The string may be out of tune. If a string has gone out of tune, it may have a decreased amount of tension, and will therefore sound worse. Bring all the strings up to the proper pitch as listed on page 69.

- The string may need to develop a light covering of rosin. If you continue to play the instrument, you may notice a subtle buildup of residue on the strings. I have found that a moderate amount of rosin can help the strings play more evenly.

- The string may have built up too much rosin. Just as in the previous example of not having enough rosin, the converse can also be true. If a string sounds funny or off, and it has an excessive amount of rosin built up on the surface, you may need to wipe it clean with either a dry cloth, or in extreme cases, a cloth lightly dampened with rubbing alcohol. (Alcohol is capable of marring some wood finishes, so use care.) In the future, use less rosin on the bow.

- Try adjusting the angle that you hold the bow. Tip it almost flat on top of the psaltery, or try it more vertically and experiment with different angles and techniques.

- You may be using too little or too much pressure on the strings. As a general rule, *the lower-pitched strings sound best with more pressure from the bow, and the higher-pitched strings need less pressure.* To help practice using the correct amount of pressure, try playing the higher-pitched strings with the far end of the bow for lighter pressure, and the lower-pitched notes with the base end or heel of the bow to create more pressure. If you have a violin bow, adjusting to a higher hair tension can help you get more pressure too.

- The strings may have been bowed at the wrong position between the pins. Typically, this occurs on the lowest notes, toward the tip of the psaltery. Lower notes should be bowed as far away from the hitch pin as possible. (Refer to the diagram on the next page.)

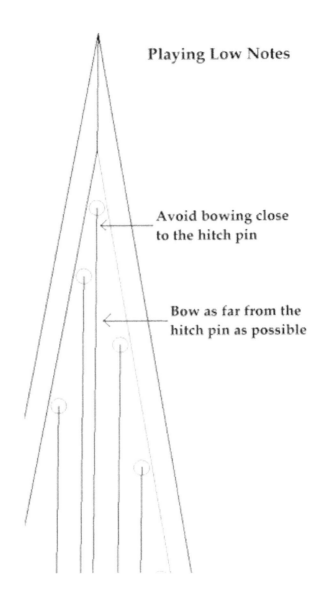

Playing Low Notes

Avoid bowing close
to the hitch pin

Bow as far from the
hitch pin as possible

Playing Songs:

Once you seem to be getting consistently good sounds from your psaltery, and have become familiar with all the notes, (this is where you might realize how helpful those note markers we put in really are), and all the ins and outs, it's time to finally make some music.

Playing songs can be done any number of ways, depending on how "music literate" you are. If you can read sheet music, you should have no trouble playing just about anything you can get your hands on.

There are a few good sheet music resources online, depending on your musical interests:

- **For folk music**, there is *The Mudcat Café.* (www.mudcat.org)

Here, you can download a program called *"The Digital Tradition: Folk Music Database."* All of the entries in this database have lyrics, and a majority of them also show you the sheet music for the song, and will play the basic tune to help you recognize and remember it.

- **For hymns and gospel music,** there is *The Cyber Hymnal.* (www.cyberhymnal.org)

This online hymnal is quite exhaustive, but in order to view most hymns as sheet music, you will also need to download a free viewer program from Noteworthy Software (www.noteworthysoftware.com).

- **For classical music,** there is the *Werner-Icking Music Archive.* (www.daimi.au.dk/~reccmo/).

WIMA has a large collection of classical music, arranged by composer, and is also searchable within the site via a search engine.

Beyond sheet music, there are all sorts of alternative music-learning programs: tabs, learn-by-number, learn-by-letter, etc. I think that each person may have their own personal learning style; and while one person may say, *"it worked for me!"* another may learn music in a completely different way. Some people just play songs by ear. Chances are, if you know a tune very well, you can probably figure it out on the bowed psaltery simply by trial and error.

Regardless of the learning technique you chose, it's useful to remember that the bowed psaltery is a *musical* instrument. You have not made piles of sawdust and wood shavings, and spent hours of finishing and stringing simply to have a decorative triangular box. Within this "box" is a song that is waiting to burst out into the air at your fingertips: all you have to do is pick up the bow and practice.

Remember to put the *bowed* in bowed psaltery, and *go make some music!*

Care and Maintenance

Taking care of a bowed psaltery can best be summed up in a few simple rules and common-sense guidelines.

Being made primarily out of wood, bowed psalteries should be kept from the elements whenever possible. This would include rain, high heat (i.e., inside a hot car), and swings in humidity; of the most troublesome is not *temperature* extremes, but rather, *humidity* swings.

Wood is hygroscopic, meaning that it will readily take in or release moisture from the air. It is this moisture change, (both gaining and losing) that is responsible for swelling and shrinking wood—even more so than temperature changes.

It's recommended that all care be taken to keep the environment where the instrument is kept as stable as possible. Try to keep the psaltery away from heat registers or windowsills, or any other area where environmental extremes may occur.

One of the best possible ways to protect your instrument from outside changes is by storing it in a case. Keeping your instrument covered and in a case, or at the very least stored away—especially during severe weather—can go a long way in preventing any possible damage to the instrument. Any changes in humidity will occur much slower when the instrument is safely stored than if it had been left out in the open.

Cleaning:

As for actually cleaning the instrument, any mild household cleaners should be sufficient for the back and sides, provided they are not too aggressive. Compatibility with any given cleaner will vary depending upon which type of finish you've applied. For instance, since shellac is an evaporative finish that's dissolved in alcohol, using any cleaner that contains alcohol will mar the finish. Any evaporative finish can be re-dissolved, (and thereby damaged), by the solvent that was originally used to store it.

In contrast, a reactive finish such as polyurethane will be incredibly resilient to all sorts of chemicals and cleaners. In a reactive finish, not only does the solvent evaporate, but also afterward the components in the finish begin a chemical reaction changing their structure; this renders the finish more durable, and unable to be re-dissolved in the solvent that was originally used to store it.

The only downside to reactive finishes is that they can't be repaired or "touched up" as easily as evaporative finishes. That is, if a finish made of shellac or lacquer gets damaged, you can simply reapply the finish in a problem area, and the new finish will melt into the existing finish, becoming one amalgamated film. However, a reactive finish will remain separate from the finish's previous film layer.

Dusting the Top:

For the top of the instrument, it can be difficult to clean in between the strings with most common cleaning implements. Some feather dusters can reach between the strings, but I've found a long-bristled paintbrush to be among the best tools for dusting off the top of a bowed psaltery.

A long-bristled paintbrush will reach beneath the strings for cleaning

Try to find a brush with soft, fine, natural bristles. There are many unsuitable brushes with hard, coarse bristles that may scratch the finish. Make gentle sweeps starting from the front of the bridge up toward the soundhole. Next, move from the tip of the psaltery down towards the bridge. If you make outward motions toward the end of the psaltery, bristles of the brush may get wedged underneath the strings where they meet the hitch pins.

The music wire itself shouldn't need much in the way of cleaning, but if any strings should become dirty or rusty, gently wipe the affected strings up and down with extra fine steel wool, (designated by the numbers 000 or 0000 wool). Sometimes this can become necessary if there is a lot of rosin buildup on the strings.

If the string was rusty, you can use any rust inhibitor, (such as WD-40), after the wire has been cleaned by spraying it first into a cloth, and then gently wiping it onto the string. Take care to keep any treatment away from the area that is actually bowed.

If it should happen that a string becomes bent, damaged, or rusted to the point where it can't be salvaged or cleaned, you'll have to replace the string.

Appendix (A)—A Brief Discussion on Pinblock Woods:

You'll notice in the chapter on making the frame, (page 16), that hard maple is recommended as the preferred wood to be used for the pinblock. So, why use hard maple?

For one, it's hard, (hence the name). It's dense enough that the fibers of the wood can hold up to the constant turning and wear of the tuning pins. Using a wood that is too soft will wear the threads in the pinblock holes prematurely and fail to hold the pins in place.

But if density were the only criterion, then ebony would be ideal for a pinblock, (which it is not). Consider a pinblock's function: we'll be drilling twenty five 3/16" holes in our pinblock, (essentially turning the pinblock into Swiss-cheese), and threading all 25 tuning pins into it. The threads on a tuning pin are very shallow, and the hole is of course drilled slightly undersized to account for these threads.

Maple has just the right *give* to slightly expand and help grab the pin as it's being driven in. With denser woods, some are so absolutely stubborn that there is almost no *give* at all, and a bigger hole has to be drilled to avoid cracking the wood. There is much less forgiveness in regards to hole sizes with some of the super-dense woods such as ebony.

> *And as a side-note: if you do end up using a very dense wood for the* ***sides*** *of your psaltery, (which is perfectly acceptable), you'll want to drill slightly oversized holes for the* ***hitch*** *pins to avoid splitting the sides. In such instances, where dense hardwoods are used for the sides, the hitch pins can act as a splitting wedge when they are inserted, and can cause the sides to split lengthwise. I use a #10 drill bit for these instances, which is .1935" in diameter, and gives the sides a little bit of extra breathing room. The* ***pinblock,*** *of course, should still be made of hard maple—and drilled with 3/16" diameter holes.*

Another thing to take into account is the grain and porosity of the wood. Hard maple has a very fine grain and small even pores, which help maximize the actual amount of wood that is in contact with the threads of the pin. Taking this one step further, some piano manufacturers even use pinblocks of laminated hard maple—sort of like a specialized plywood. These pinblocks are made of very thin laminations of maple or beech to ensure complete evenness and consistency throughout the block.

One helpful thing to keep in mind is this: if you can't find hard maple in a full 1½" thickness, there is absolutely nothing wrong with gluing two or more thinner pieces together to reach the full thickness. (Just be sure that the layers are stacked horizontally, not vertically; otherwise, a tight tuning pin might split the layers apart.)

Another point is what I would call wood "oiliness." Some woods are dense, but they are also very oily too, especially rosewoods. This would seem to suggest that they would be more prone to slipping, or maybe even the opposite with some woods—sticking, if the pins get gummed up with tree resins. Also, many darker woods have a high amount of tannin, which may cause premature corrosion of the tuning pins as well. (This is much less critical for the *sides* of the psaltery because the hitch pins are stationary and do not rely on the threads to make any adjustments.)

Also, there is the matter of *stability*. The two primary factors to consider are: moisture content and grain pattern. The pinblock wood should be dry and straight-grained. Try to avoid wood that has knots, curl, spalt, bird's-eye, or anything out of the ordinary. The crucial thing to remember is consistency and homogeny. Also, wood that has not been dried thoroughly will want to warp and twist as it dries—hopefully not while it's holding all the tuning pins on your psaltery. The general rule of thumb on freshly cut lumber for air-drying is to wait one year per inch of thickness. (Or just buy lumber that has been kiln-dried for you.)

All this to say: I highly recommend using hard maple for your pinblock. This wood, from the tree *Acer saccharum*, goes by many names: hard maple, sugar maple, or rock maple. If you are buying maple, I would make sure that it is specifically *hard maple*, by either one of the three names listed above, as there are many types of soft maple commonly available as well, and can easily be confused.

Now, I recognize that some will be making this on a shoestring budget, and not everyone will be able to get a piece of hard maple in all situations. Additionally, there are numerous types of trees and lumber worldwide, with different species available in different locales. So, if for whatever reason(s) you can't buy a hard maple pinblock, here are some alternatives:

- If you are in Europe, then European Beech is an excellent choice, and is almost regarded as the European equivalent to hard maple. (Some even consider it superior to hard maple.)

- There are certain domestic species that can work with varying degrees of success: ash, walnut, and red or white oak. (If in doubt about a wood's density, you can give it the fingernail test—try gouging your fingernail into an edge of the board and see if it leaves a nick. Hard maple will only leave the faintest of marks, if any at all.)

I would say though, please, for your own sake, avoid using woods on the extreme ends of the hardness spectrum for the pinblock. On the soft side, stay away from pine, cedar, redwood, fir, spruce, as well as any of the softer hardwoods, like aspen or poplar. On the harder side, avoid the extremely hard and "stubborn" exotic hardwoods that may very well crack if given only ³⁄₁₆" diameter holes for the tuning pins; these woods include: bloodwood, ebony, purpleheart, wenge, and most rosewoods.

Appendix (B)—Glues Used in Making Musical Instruments:

Not all glues that are popular for woodworking are necessarily the best for instrument making—and especially not the best for making a bowed psaltery. The objectives and goals are slightly different in the two situations; while it's true that in both instances the goal is to stick two pieces of wood together, some other questions arise:

> *Was this glue designed to withstand several hundred pounds of continuous pressure pulling against the joint?*

> *Will this glue come apart when exposed to high heat or humidity (as in the inside of a hot car)?*

I think you get the picture. While there have been all sorts of advances made in woodworking glues for making things like furniture and crafts, (i.e., water resistance, extended open-time, and colored glues), many of these very same specialty glues are among the worst for making musical instruments.

One of the most important factors in musical instrument building, and psalteries specifically, is *creep resistance*. That is to say: *creep* is a glue's tendency to slowly pull apart when put under a continuous load, as is the case with a bowed psaltery.

So with exterior and waterproof wood glues, (like Titebond II and Titebond III), which are great for building furniture, their special water-resistance additives and other attributes frequently come at the cost of creep resistance. Supposedly, chemicals added to the glue can inhibit them from fully hardening, and this therefore decreases their longevity when put under a constant load.

Just what glues can/should be used for building a bowed psaltery?

In all honesty, you can really use just about any/all types of glues, even ones like Titebond, with varying degrees of success. A lot will depend on how well you have joined the frame and top/bottom together. Some glues are more forgiving than others at filling small gaps between the pieces to be joined. (When I rate how good a specific glue is at *gap filling,* I'm not rating how good it is at simply filling in the gap, but how much *strength* it is actually able to impart when bridging that gap. It has nothing to do with aesthetics and everything to do with strength.)

Nonetheless, using the right kind of glue (and understanding how to use it properly) can go a long way in increasing the strength and longevity of your psaltery. Some glues that I've either used personally, or have heard to be good in regards to creep resistance are:

- **Polyurethane-based glues (Gorilla Glue, Ultimate Glue, etc.)** — Widely available at most hardware and woodworking stores. When using this glue, it's important that you moisten both surfaces of the wood with water just before gluing; this moisture helps activate the glue. Also, polyurethane glue expands as it cures, so you need to have the pieces firmly clamped together or they may move apart during the curing process. (Polyurethane glue is not water-based, and therefore can be messy to clean off your hands and clothes.) The curing process takes several hours, so plan on leaving the pieces clamped together for the better part of the day. This glue is not good at filling gaps at all, so you must take care to ensure that your joints fit together snugly when using this glue. On the upside, polyurethane-based glue is virtually impervious to heat, moisture, and creep: three very big pluses.

   (Note: polyurethane was the type of glue used to build the psaltery for this book.)

- **2-part epoxy glues (System Three, West System, etc.)** — Available at woodworking stores like Rockler and Woodcraft, (check for local stores near you), as well as most hobby stores. Epoxy requires you to mix two components: the resin and the hardener, in a prescribed ratio. If mixed and applied properly, epoxy is an excellent choice for instruments, but try to avoid the 5-minute variety. (It seems that whenever a glue is "new and improved," as with the 5-minute variety of epoxy, all of the desirable attributes for musical instrument construction are compromised.) One of the only problems that could arise with epoxy is if the mixing ratio and application instructions aren't followed. Provided you use high-quality woodworker's epoxy, this glue is probably the best choice for those who have less-than-desirable joinery work on the frame of their psaltery as it's excellent in filling gaps. However, epoxy can be relatively expensive, (for a glue), though this may be partly due to the fact that it is generally sold in large quantities.

- **Hot hide glue (granular glue dissolved in hot water)**—Available at woodworking stores, as well as some online and specialty stores. Probably one of the best glues for creep resistance, and widely used by luthiers. Hide glue requires you to dissolve the glue in a double boiler glue pot full of hot water. One of the trademarks of this glue is that it's reversible with heat/humidity—a handy feature for builders of guitars or violins when they need to pop the top off and adjust something inside the instrument—though this isn't something that is of much value on a bowed psaltery, as there are scores of pins and strings on the top, and in my opinion, should be constructed permanently. But for everything that you ever wanted to know about hide glue, visit www.frets.com and navigate to the page dedicated to hide glue. I wouldn't recommend hide glue to beginners because it requires more experience to use properly, and it's not good at filling gaps in joinery.

- **Titebond Original (sometimes called "yellow glue")**—This is the most common glue used by many woodworkers, and it's what most people think of when they say "wood glue." It's widely available at hardware and woodworking stores. You can also use any other yellow glue like Elmer's, as long as it's an interior wood glue—plain, ordinary wood glue, with no fancy additives. The plainer, the better. Yellow glue can still creep, but can be used if you don't feel comfortable with any of the other glues listed above. A lot will depend on how good your joinery has been. I specifically use the Titebond brand glue for various tasks (except gluing frames) because it's the most trusted and reliable among the woodworkers that I've talked to.

- **Luthier's Mercantile International instrument glue**—This is just another formulation of wood glue, though it's held in high regard among some instrument builders. As I understand it, this glue supposedly does not contain the yellow dye found in other wood glues, (it's actually white), and is therefore purer and dries harder than standard wood glue. In theory then, it should be more resistant to creep, though it still won't hold up as well as the glues listed at the top of this list. This glue can only be found from one source: the Luthier's Mercantile International website (www.lmii.com).

- **Cyanoacrylate glues (Hot Stuff, USA Gold, etc.)**—Available in some hardware stores as "Super glue" or "Krazy glue"—though most of the higher quality types are only found in woodworking and hobby stores. To be honest, I only use Cyanoacrylate (abbreviated CA) glues for gluing small things like inlays and decorations. I don't have any experience with this glue in terms of the structural gluing of an instrument, but supposedly it has very good creep resistance. If you're a woodworker who has a decent amount of experience with this type of glue, it may be worth your while to try it; though I can't really comment much on CA glues for this application.

In my opinion, there really isn't any one "perfect" glue, but each person uses what works best for their situation. Epoxy will do the best job in making up for deficiencies in joinery, but nothing can bail you out of complete sloppiness.

The heart of the matter is this: use good joinery—to the best of your abilities. Don't rush through things. And, if you still can't get the joints perfect, at the very least read and follow the manufacturer's instructions carefully for any of the glues—you don't want to compound the problem.

One last thing that you can consider if you've glued your frame together and you're worried about its long-term integrity: use lighter gauge strings to minimize the pull on the frame. Please refer to page 55 within the chapter on stringing for more information.

Appendix (C)—Why Soundboards are Made of Quartersawn Softwoods:

Now, in contrast with the back, the top has the important job of transferring the strings' vibrations, and passing them on to the rest of the instrument. I think of the top as only a *passer*, and the back as the one that *holds* the sound—though we can use different kinds of passers to influence what types of sounds are being transferred. For this job, we try to employ the lightest wood possible, (usually a softwood such as cedar or spruce), so that as little of the vibrations as possible are held by the soundboard, but are instead passed on to the rest of the instrument's body. The more of these vibrations that can fully reach and sound over the entire body of the psaltery, the fuller the sound will become—at least in theory.

Here is my theory as to why some psaltery builders use hardwoods for the soundboard: the sides are so thick, that so little vibrations make it to the back anyway. Accordingly, the job of the back (resonating the vibrations) is instead accomplished by the top. The back becomes almost irrelevant, and the whole flow of vibrations is contained mainly within just the top and sides. The big drawback to all of this is that the depth of the tone is greatly compromised. The tone of the strings *sound* good, but it is also *shallow*. It's like a beautiful photograph: it looks good, but it's only two-dimensional with no depth.

My building philosophy is much different: I want all the strings' vibrations to shoot down throughout the entire body of the instrument, maximizing the eventual projection of these vibrations out the soundhole. I go about pursuing this goal and adjusting my building plans in a few different ways; the main ways include minimizing the thickness of the sides, and using a wood of low mass for the top.

As a side-note to all of this, even the Israelites from thousands of years ago knew to use wood of a low mass for building their musical instruments. I found this quote interesting, (fir is a softwood similar to spruce and pine).

*"And David and all the house of Israel played before the LORD on all manner of **instruments made of fir wood,** even on harps, and on psalteries, and on timbrels, and on cornets, and on cymbals."* -2 Samuel 6:5

Now, as a balance to this, we also need a piece of wood that is strong enough to hold up to the pressure created from all 25 of the strings. In other stringed instruments, this usually involves bracing the underside of the soundboard in one way or another. With a bowed psaltery, most builders chose to simply position the bridge close to the pinblock, with the bridge ends also resting on the sides of the instrument for added support. (Though I think that adding bracing similar to that found on a guitar or lute is a good idea for psalteries under some circumstances.)

But closely related to strength is also *stability*. Wood absorbs and releases moisture in the air depending on the humidity level until an equilibrium is reached. When the wood absorbs moisture, it expands, and when it loses moisture, it contracts.

Quartersawn wood is wood that has been cut with the tree's growth rings running at 90° vertical (or close to it) when viewed on the end, while flat-sawn wood can have the growth rings in just about any orientation that happens to come up when cutting a log—usually at a lower angle.

On top are three pieces of quartersawn redwood, while the maple below is flat-sawn

Because of the way that wood gains and loses moisture, the orientation of the growth rings plays a major part in the wood's stability. Along its width, quartersawn wood expands only about half as much as flat-sawn wood. Also, for quartersawn boards, the manner in which it expands is also very uniform—it tends to stay flat. Conversely, flat-sawn boards move unevenly, and can twist and cup. This is most dramatic and pronounced in thinner woods—such as the ones used for soundboards.

In making musical instruments, these changes may be very slight—maybe even undetectable to the eye at times—but to the wood, it's very critical. The back of the psaltery can deform or warp slightly under adverse conditions if it's flat-sawn. But if the top tries to shrink, expand, or warp— with the bridge and the weight of all the strings bearing down on it—the wood is doubly stressed and restricted in its movement, and may crack. Because of this, quartersawn wood is almost always used for the tops of acoustic musical instruments.

Appendix (D)—Soundhole Sizing and the Helmholtz Resonator

I will readily admit that I don't understand all of the physics and principles behind the Helmholtz resonator, simply that the following is the method that I personally use to find how large to make a soundhole. What I admit that I do know is that this method seems to be better than a completely blind guess. I've used it thus far with good results—though that certainly doesn't mean it's the best or only method to calculate soundhole sizes.

First, a little background, as well as I understand it:

In the 1860s, a very gifted German scientist and physicist named Hermann von Helmholtz created, (among many other things), a device known today as a *Helmholtz resonator*. It was basically a spherical jug tapering off to a small hole meant to be used for the purpose of studying the resonance of air contained within a cavity—similar to the whistling effect when blowing air across the spout of a big glass jug.

As it has been explained to me, according to Helmholtz's work, in order to maximize the sound volume of such a resonator (sphere), the ideal opening size (in terms of its radius) should be equal to ¼ of the overall radius of the sphere.

Basically, what we have to do is calculate the total volume inside the psaltery, and then calculate how large a sphere would be that has an identical volume. Then, we simply take the radius of that theoretical sphere, and divide by four. This number will then be the size of the radius for the supposedly ideal soundhole—at least in terms of maximum decibel volume.

So, let's begin with our current psaltery—I hope you're not afraid of a little math! It can't be too tough, it's a simple triangle, where area is equal to its base times its height, divided by two: **a = (b × h ÷ 2)**

So, taking some *inside* measurements of the psaltery, I got: (in inches)

Psaltery length = **18 ⁹⁄₁₆**
Psaltery width = **6 ⁹⁄₁₆**

Therefore, **6 ⁹⁄₁₆ × 18 ⁹⁄₁₆ ÷ 2 = ~60.9 in²** for the surface area of the inside of the psaltery.

From there, we just multiply by the depth of the psaltery (1½ inches) to get the overall volume.

So, **~60.9 in² × 1½ = ~91.36 in³** for the overall volume of the soundbox.

Now, to convert this volume measurement into that of a sphere, it gets a little bit tricky. The formula for finding the volume of a sphere is $v = \frac{4}{3}\pi \times r^3$

Now, rearranging things and solving for **r**, we get the following equation:

$r = (v \div \frac{4}{3}\pi)^{\frac{1}{3}}$

So, we take the number we got for the volume of the psaltery, (**91.36 in³**) and plug it in as **v** in our equation.

First we divide our volume calculation by $\frac{4}{3}\pi$, or **~4.1888**, and get **21.811**

Next, find the cube root, which means $21.811^{\frac{1}{3}}$

And we get **~2.79"**

In a nutshell, the volume of our psaltery is equal to the volume of a sphere with a radius of **2.79** inches. And now for the final payoff, dividing by four to get the size of the soundhole: **2.79" ÷ 4 = .6975"**

So, the ideal soundhole size for this instrument is a circle with a radius of **.6975** inches, or a diameter of **1.395** inches.

Overall, a **1⅜" (1.375")** hole would do nicely. Now, you'll notice that I used a *triangular* soundhole so it will help to know the *surface area* of our ideal hole size, which can be found with the following equation: $a = \pi r^2$

$.6975^2 \times \pi = {\sim}1.528 \text{ in}^2$

So the number we are shooting for is a surface area of about **1.5 in²**, which can be used for any shape you want to carve into the soundboard. For the triangle, it was pretty simple, as $a = (b \times h \div 2)$, so a simple **1" x 3"** triangle would have an area of exactly **1.5 in²**—close enough for me!

Now, I don't know how reliable any of this all is, but it seems like a good starting point. If you were to start with an instrument with no soundhole, and gradually enlarge it, the sound would get louder and louder. Eventually it would top-out and start getting quieter again. (Imagine a giant 5" hole in the top of our psaltery!) This is the best way that I know of to find the ideal soundhole size.

One last thought—even if the equation gets us very close to the ideal soundhole size in terms of *volume*, would this really be ideal? Is volume all that we're concerned with? It's claimed that smaller soundholes help accentuate the trebles, while larger ones favor the bass end. That is a gross generalization though; you can experiment if you want, and find what you think works best.

Appendix (E) — Why Varying String Gauges are Used on Musical Instruments:

A string's gauge (thickness) is directly related to its tension. The thicker the string, the more tension it will exert on the instrument, all other things being equal.

Tension is calculated through three things:

- **Pitch** of the string
- **Length** of the string
- **Mass** of the string

On a bowed psaltery that we've already built, we can't change the string's prescribed *pitch*, (unless we want a terrible sounding instrument!) or the *length*, so the only way to change the amount of tension on the string is by manipulating its *mass*.

Why would we want to change the amount of tension on a string? Well, one useful measurement is called the tension-to-length ratio: this measures how many pounds of tension is on the string per inch. But in the real world, what it actually measures is how tight or loose the string feels.

If the T/L ratio is low, (as is usually the case on the lowest-pitched, and longest strings), the strings will feel very loose. Likewise, if the T/L ratio is high, (common on the shortest strings), the strings will feel very stiff and rigid. A change in this ratio will also change the properties of how the string sounds. The string will still be in tune, but it will sound *different* — *m*aybe stiff, or maybe weak or thin, or a number of other things. (I will readily admit that I don't fully understand all of the subtleties of music strings in this area.)

We vary the thickness of the strings in order to even out the ratio of the tension and to normalize some of the strings' tonal qualities. If the shortest and the longest strings both have the same (thin) gauge of wire and the same amount of tension, that means that the longest string will feel much looser than the shortest string. Even though the overall tension on both strings is the same, there will be very little *downward* pressure on the longest string: it won't make strong contact with the bridge, and its vibrations won't drive the soundboard and reach the rest of the instrument as well as the shorter strings.

To compensate for this, we can gradually increase the string gauges so that the longest string will at least have a decent amount of tension spread across the string. Similarly, we can also reduce the gauge of the shortest strings so they don't feel quite so tight.

In nearly all instances, we cannot completely even out all the tension and get a perfectly balanced tension-to-length ratio, but we can usually avoid any extremes on each end of the psaltery. This helps keep the tone sounding even and more consistent as you progress down the strings.

Now, on our sample psaltery, I would normally vary the string gauge from .010" to .014" across the entire instrument, but I have instead chosen to use a middle gauge—.012" diameter—as a good in-between wire for the sake of simplicity. This prevents too large of an extreme from occurring at either end of the psaltery. Since this is only a 2-octave psaltery, there is not that much of a spread of lengths between the strings anyway. The biggest diversity occurs when the strings get both very long and very short.

Now, to help clear up a few *misconceptions* about string gauge:

Thicker string gauges are not used to stretch the range of pitches lower, and thinner string gauges are not used to stretch an instrument's range higher. String gauge has very little, if anything, to do with the available range on a psaltery.

An exception to this is over-wound strings—common on other stringed instruments—which is a whole different animal. Hereafter I'll focus only on solid music wire in this section; but briefly, an over-wound string has a layer of outer winding that's meant to artificially inflate the mass of the string, (one of the three variables listed on page 110 that can influence a string's tension). Yet, the winding doesn't really contribute to the string's strength, thereby allowing it to sound at a lower frequency while maintaining the same amount of tension.

But underneath the outer windings, these strings have the very same gauges and sizes of music wire as those that are commonly used in the stringing of bowed psalteries. The core wires are *the very same*, and adhere to the very same universal principles as regular music wire: it's just that wound strings are much more complex, using any number of materials (bronze, copper, steel, etc.) for the outer windings.

But getting back to the discussion at hand: making a plain steel string thicker doesn't allow it go any higher or lower in pitch than it normally could. This may seem counter-intuitive, but try to follow:

If you make a string thicker, it's much stronger and will break at a higher tension. But, this increase in strength is offset *exactly* by an increase in mass, which is self-defeating. The string is still made of the exact same material, just more of it. In a nutshell, a thicker string is strong and can handle more tension, but it will also take that much more tension to bring that thicker string up to the same note.

On the flipside, making a string thinner doesn't make it any weaker—at a given pitch—than a thicker string. Remember, on a psaltery the pitch and length of the string are both fixed. A thinner wire has a lower breaking point, but the wire also will require a proportionately equal reduction in tension to be tuned to the same note as a thicker wire made of the same material.

One minor exception to this is steel music wire—because of the way it is made—which has a slightly higher tensile strength at thinner gauges. This increase is mostly negligible within the small variances of diameters used in psalteries, but pound for pound, the strongest wire is actually the *thinnest!*

To help illustrate these points, let's take a look at a real-world example, with calculations taken from an actual psaltery:

The string E_6 (1,318 Hz) on a psaltery is exactly 7 inches long. It is strung with a .010" diameter string. Assuming a tensile strength of 387,000 PSI for this steel string, this means that the breaking point of the wire itself is about 30.39 pounds. ($\pi r^2 \times$ *Tensile Strength = Breaking Point.*) Since it's tuned to 1318 Hz, there is about 19.6 pounds of tension on this string. At the current setup, this string is at about 64.5 percent of its breaking point. (And its $T\!/\!L$ ratio is 2.8 pounds per inch, which is good.)

Now, let's see what happens when we put a heavier string on and keep it tuned to the same pitch. We'll go up to a .014" steel string—since it's the same material, the tensile strength is still at 387,000 PSI. The string therefore has a breaking point of nearly double what our thinner wire had—a whopping 59.57 pounds for the breaking point! Now, accordingly, it's also that much thicker too, and it will take a full 38.4 pounds to bring this hefty string up to the frequency of E_6 (1318 Hz.) With the current setup, this bigger, tougher, stronger string is still stuck at 64.5 percent of the string's breaking point. (And the $T\!/\!L$ ratio has been raised to around 5.5 pounds per inch, which is rather high.)

And here's another kicker: that thicker .014" wire—which was assumed to have an equal tensile strength of 387,000 PSI (on average)—is actually a tad bit weaker due to how steel music wire is manufactured. It's more like 369,000 PSI (average) tensile strength, so the breaking point is really closer to 56.9 pounds. So in reality, the 38.4 pounds of pressure we needed to bring it up to pitch was stressing the string at close to 67.5 percent of its limit, not 64.5 percent.

Basically, string gauges are used to control tension and the $T\!/\!L$ ratio, not an instrument's playable range. When dealing with steel music wire, the *vibrating length* of the string is what determines its range. (This is also partially why the neck on a bass guitar is longer than a regular guitar.)

Appendix (F)—Why Even Hitch Pin Spacing Doesn't Work Well:

First off, it will be helpful to gain a basic understanding of the different pitches that make up our common music notes. Any given musical pitch is simply a series of vibrations, measured in how many of these vibrations occur per second, called hertz. The standard that is commonly used today is based on the first A above middle C being tuned to 440 hertz.

Listed below are the notes and frequencies of all 25 strings that are used in making our Psimple Psaltery:

Note	Frequency	Note	Frequency
G_4	392.00	G_5	783.99
$G^{\#}_4/A^{b}_4$	415.30	$G^{\#}_5/A^{b}_5$	830.61
A_4	440.00	A_5	880.00
$A^{\#}_4/B^{b}_4$	466.16	$A^{\#}_5/B^{b}_5$	932.33
B_4	493.88	B_5	987.77
C_5	523.25	C_6	1,046.50
$C^{\#}_5/D^{b}_5$	554.37	$C^{\#}_6/D^{b}_6$	1,108.73
D_5	587.33	D_6	1,174.66
$D^{\#}_5/E^{b}_5$	622.25	$D^{\#}_6/E^{b}_6$	1,244.51
E_5	659.26	E_6	1,318.51
F_5	698.46	F_6	1,396.91
$F^{\#}_5/G^{b}_5$	739.99	$F^{\#}_6/G^{b}_6$	1,479.98
		G_6	1,567.98

Take a look at the lowest note—G_4. This is the first G above middle C. (Middle C is not listed, but has a frequency of 261.63 Hz.) Now look at the difference between G_4 and the next whole note, A_4. It jumps from 392 Hz up to 440 Hz. That's a jump of 48 Hz.

Next, go up one full octave to G_5, and compare G_5 to A_5. It goes from 783.99 Hz to 880.00 Hz. That's a jump of: 48 Hz again? Nope. It's actually *double*, at just over 96 Hz difference.

So, what am I trying to say with all of this? What should be understood is that *musical pitches change at an uneven pace.* If you ever see a guitar player, look closely at the frets, (the little wire bars that run along the neck of the instrument), and you'll notice that the frets are spaced *unevenly.* The frets at the top are spaced much wider than the frets at the bottom. This is a good way to visualize how the frequency of musical notes changes at an uneven pace.

On a guitar, the frets must be placed in exactly the right proportions in order for the notes to sound at the right pitch—all the notes are played on that one string, with a fixed amount of tension for all the possible pitches. Now with a bowed psaltery, it's a bit different: we don't have to get the pins in the exact right place, because if we're off by a little bit, we can compensate by tuning each individual string's tension up or down so that it's still playing the right note.

So in effect, when we miss this mark, we get just a little bit off from the length that the string really wants to be vibrating at. If we miss the first pin by only ⅛" from this ideal, it will be no big deal, and probably won't be noticed. The problem creeps up when we keep on missing this mark, and the errors accumulate and become greater and greater. Soon we're off by ¼", and then by ⅜", and then before you know it, by the last strings, the spacing is off by several inches.

When strings get stretched *too far* beyond this ideal, they still sound good, but they tend to break frequently. When strings *fall short* of this ideal, they give a scratchy or metallic sound which gets worse depending on how far they are away from the ideal.

The general rule of thumb is that this acoustic ideal is about ⅔ (66 percent) of a string's breaking point; too far over that, and the string is too close to breaking; too far below, and tone will be compromised. Of course, on different instruments, depending on if the strings are plucked or bowed, or very high or very low, these rules can be bent a little. Usually lower strings are more forgiving than higher strings regarding shortness, but bowed strings are much more picky than plucked strings in staying near this number—they need fairly high tension.

Now, let me give some specific, real-world examples and numbers. It will help to show you this graphically.

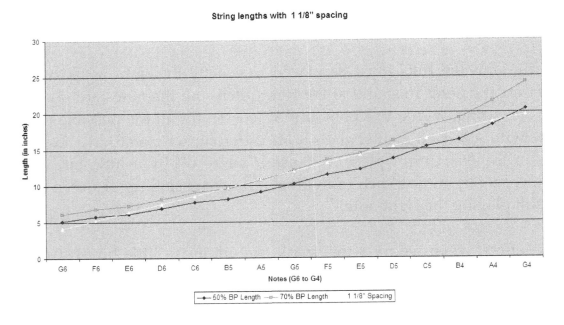

I've taken all the 25 notes listed above for our bowed psaltery project, and charted out two points: 70 percent of the string's breaking point (what I consider to be the highest safe point) and 50 percent of the string's breaking point (what I consider to be the minimum to have the string still sound acceptable.) Along with this, I've charted a hypothetical stringing arrangement that a builder might use: 1⅛" equal spacing between all pins on the right-hand side of the psaltery.

Looking at the 50 and 70 percent breaking point lines—the upper and lower limits of the strings—you'll notice sort of a tunnel. In order to create a successful psaltery—that is to say, one that does not have any strings with a dangerously high tension, nor a tension that is too low—I feel that you have to stay within this tunnel. Notice how this tunnel is not *straight*, but it *curves upward*? The ideal lengths of strings do not increase evenly, but they get longer at *an increasing pace*. When we string a psaltery with even spacing, this effectively limits us to drawing a straight line through this tunnel.

Now, in this situation we see our 2-octave psaltery using strings that are spaced evenly at 1⅛" between pins. (Refer to the graph on the previous page.) The middle and long notes around G5 to G4 are great, and everything seems to be going well until we get to the shortest few notes. Notice on G6 and F6 how the stringing line falls below our lower limit? These strings, kept at this length, will sound rather crummy.

High notes are especially sensitive to tension—and just look at how narrow the tunnel becomes on the left side of the graph! I would even venture to guess that the first 3 highest notes will sound bad, and the fourth will probably be hit-or miss depending on how your bow hits the string. The tension is just too low—the strings need to be longer in order to increase the tension for these notes.

Now, let's take another example, still using even hitch pin spacing:

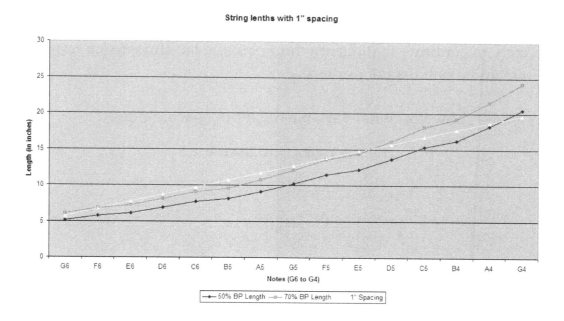

In the above example, we've kept the longest string (G4) the same length, (this string determines the length of the psaltery, so we won't be able to change this string unless we make the actual instrument longer), but we've changed the spacing from 1⅛" between pins down to 1". This effectively takes our center line and swivels it upward with G4 as our pivot point. Now, the lowest notes will sound good; actually, all the notes should sound good in this example. (Remember that the lowest notes aren't nearly as picky as the high ones, and we can fudge the rules just a bit on the lower half.)

There is just one problem with this hypothetical psaltery: look at the stringing line over the notes E_6 to G_5—busted! B_5 is *really* busted! Many of these strings are very close to their breaking points, approaching 90 percent of their maximum tension. These strings will really be prone to breaking, especially if you accidentally tune the string a half-step too high, or if there is humid weather—causing the frame to expand. These strings will probably break often and will need to be replaced regularly.

Just looking closely at our arcing tunnel, you may realize that it is *not possible* to really come up with a stringing scheme that will span the entire distance and still be in the tunnel. Go ahead and try it yourself—hold a sheet of paper or a ruler up to the graph, and try to make a straight line that falls within the tunnel. It can't be done—and this is just with a 2-octave psaltery! Imagine how much the problems would be compounded if we were to continue that narrow tunnel to the left three to six more notes for a two and a half octave psaltery.

Now, let me show you what variable hitch pin spacing does:

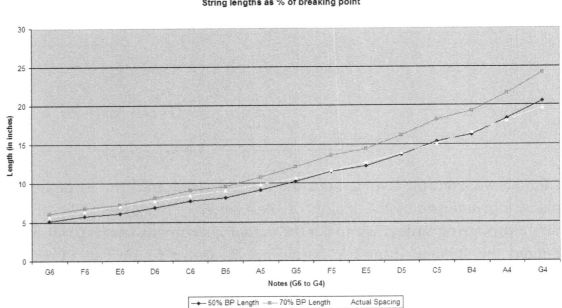

The highest notes hug the upper limit line, as they are the most sensitive to tension. From there, when we start to get close to the 50 percent line, *we gradually change the spacing.* What this does, in effect, is put a nice bend in our spacing line.

Voilà! Our stringing suddenly fits in the tunnel! And not only that, but since we can bend the line in different places, and at different rates, we are also able to break past our 2-octave barrier if we want. (Shown on the previous page is the actual spacing used on the psaltery for this book.)

That's it, in a nutshell. Though I admit, this is a somewhat simplified version, minus all the math and physics! There are a lot more variables that weren't discussed, but the principles are hopefully clear.

Appendix (G)—Material Densities

Designing a bowed psaltery (or any musical instrument for that matter) requires you to be a bit of a scientist—or even a bit of a mathematician or physicist at times. While not everyone likes this aspect of lutherie—usually those that like to stick strictly to the prescribed plans or make exact replicas of instruments—I tend to enjoy this "research and development" phase. Accordingly, one thing that's very helpful is knowing the density of any given material.

How heavy is that?

How well will it resonate a musical vibration? (for the back/sides)

How much will it impede a musical vibration? (for the soundboard/bridge)

How will it stand up to wear?

While you may not necessarily be able to get a full picture of how a given material will react simply from its density, it is a good start, and certainly better than a blind guess. So, to help measure and compare all sorts of different materials, whether they are wood, metal, plastic, or some other form, I've compiled a table of material densities.

Metals *(density listed in Kg/M³)*			
Aluminum	2,768	Nickel	8,553
Beryllium	1,868	Phosphor Bronze	8,858
Brass	8,500	Platinum	21,452
Cast Iron	6,975	Silver	10,491
Chromium	7,197	Stainless Steel	7,861
Copper	8,940	Steel	7,861
Gold	18,878	Tin	7,308
Lead	11,349	Titanium	4,512
Magnesium	1,743	Tungsten	19,293
Molybdenum	10,214	Zinc	7,141

Woods *(weight listed is average dried weight in Kg/M³)*			
Acacia Blackwood	660	Lignum Vitae (Ironwood)	1,310
Ash, White	660	Mahogany, Honduran	640
Balsa	160	Mahogany, Philippine (Lauan)	382*
Basswood	420	Makore	620
Beech, European	720	Mango	570
Birch	700	Maple, Hard	720
Bloodwood	960	Maple, Soft	620
Bocote	800	Oak, Red	770
Brazilwood	1,280	Oak, White	770
Bubinga	880	Padauk	720
Butternut	450	Panga Panga	930
Cedar, Western Red	370	Pink Ivory	990
Chakte Kok	640	Poplar	450
Chechen	850	Purpleheart	930
Cherry, Black	580	Redwood	420
Cocobolo	1,040	Rosewood, Brazilian	850
Douglas Fir	520	Rosewood, East Indian	830
Ebony, African	1,000	Rosewood, Honduran	940
Ebony, Gaboon	1,193*	Sapele	620
Ebony, Macassar	1,090	Shedua	748*
Elm, American	560	Snakewood	1,295
Goncalo Alves	940	Spruce, Sitka	420
Hickory	820	Teak	640
Holly	800	Tulipwood	960
Jarrah	800	Verawood	1,218*
Jatoba	900	Walnut, Black	640
Kiaat	700*	Wenge	880
Kingwood	1,200	Yellowheart	860
Koa	660	Zebrawood	740
Kwila	963*	Ziricote	880
Lemonwood	820	*Denotes my own measurements*	

Material (*common name*)	Density (*in Kg/M³*)
Plastics	
ABS (Acrylonitrile butadiene styrene)	1,052
Acetal (Delrin)	1,356
Acrylic	1,163
Neoprene	1,384
Polyamide (Nylon)	1,100
Polycarbonate	1,190
LDPE (Low-Density Polyethylene)	913
HDPE (High-Density Polyethylene)	941
Polypropylene	913
PVC (polyvinyl chloride)	1,467
Teflon	2,159
Others	
Carbon Fiber	1,743
Human Bone	1,439
Water	1,000

This table is not meant to be exhaustive, nor is it to be seen as authoritative. For instance, there are many different types of aluminum alloys, and while I could list something like: *"Aluminum 1100, Aluminum 3003, Aluminum 6061, etc."* I've instead chosen to simplify things and simply write a good representative number for each material as a whole. I've intended for this table to be used to get a broad overview of materials, and how their densities relate to each other, and not necessarily as an in-depth reference guide.

Bibliography

Cumpiano, William, and John Natelson, *Guitarmaking, tradition and technology*. Amherst, MA, Rosewood Press, 1987.
>   *A very thorough and authoritative guide on guitarmaking; many useful insights for psalteries.*

Flexner, Bob, *Understanding Wood Finishing*. Emmaus, PA, Rodale Press, 1994.
>   *Good overview on surface preparation and wood finishing.*

Gibbs, Nick, *The Real Wood Bible*. Richmond Hill, Ont., Firefly Books, 2005.
>   *Information on wood drying, stability, density, and working properties.*

Hopkin, Bart, *Making Simple Musical Instruments*. Asheville, NC, Lark Books, 1995.
>   *Includes plans on making a bowed psaltery, among other simple instruments.*

Hopkin, Bart, *Musical Instrument Design: practical information for instrument making*. Tucson, AZ, See Sharp Press, 1996.
>   *Overview of acoustics as relating to the construction of musical instruments; brief mention of the bowed psaltery.*

Jewitt, Jeff, *Great Wood Finishes*. Newtown, CT, Taunton Press, 2000.
>   *Good information on techniques and materials in obtaining a professional finish.*

Jourdain, Joseph, *The Folk Harp Stringband*. Wells, BC, Canada, Willow River Institute, 1997.
>   *An indispensable guide for understanding string tension, length, and related acoustic properties.*

Kirby, Ian, and John Kelsey, *Making Joints*. Emmaus, PA, Rodale Press, 1996.
>   *Good information on processing and preparing lumber for joining/gluing.*

Reblitz, Arthur, *Piano Servicing, Tuning, & Rebuilding*. Vestal, NY, Vestal Press, 1976.
>   *Information on tuning, pinblock materials, and general musical instrument construction.*

Roberts, Ronald, *Making a Simple Violin and Viola*. North Pomfret, VT, David & Charles, 1975.
>   *Guide to making an experimental, simplified version of the violin. Another "simple" instrument to build.*

Saint-George, Henry, *The bow, its history, manufacture & use*. London, "The Strad" Office, 1896.
>   *A thorough history of the musical bow, showing its evolution and progression.*

Siminoff, Roger, *The Luthier's Handbook*. Milwaukee, WI, Hal Leonard Corp., 2002.
>   *A useful guide detailing the technical aspects of wood, strings, and more.*

Strobel, Henry, *Violin Making, Step by Step*. Aumsville, OR, H.A. Strobel, 1994.
>   *Good information on bowed stringed instrument construction and acoustics.*

Taylor, R. Zachary, *Making Early Stringed Instruments*, Hertford, UK, Stobart Davies, 1991.
>   *Includes brief plans on making a bowed psaltery, among other early instruments.*

Sources of Psaltery Supplies

Many of the tools and supplies needed in making a bowed psaltery can be found locally at a hardware store or hobby shop. However, certain specialty items can usually only be obtained through online vendors. Below is a listing of such sources, along with their internet address, and what each vendor offers.

ALASKA SPECIALTY WOODS
http://alaskaspecialtywoods.com/
Spruce and cedar soundboards.
Requires minimum order.

AMAZON.COM
http://www.amazon.com/
Digital tuners, tools, supplies.

CONSTANTINE'S WOOD CENTER
http://www.constantines.com/
Tools, supplies, glues, wood, and finishes.

EBAY
http://www.ebay.com/
Violin bows, exotic woods, digital tuners, woodworking hardware, et al.

ELDERLY INSTRUMENTS
http://www.elderly.com/
Music wire, zither pins, tuning wrenches, tonewood, bows, bow hair, and rosin.

FOLKCRAFT INSTRUMENTS
http://www.folkcraft.com/
Music wire, zither pins, tuning wrenches, tonewood, bows, bow hair, and rosin.

GRAINGER INDUSTRIAL SUPPLY
http://www.grainger.com/
Bridge saddles, various parts and supplies.
Many US locations for local pickup.

LEE VALLEY
http://www.leevalley.com/
Tools, supplies, glues and wood finishes.

LUTHIERS MERCANTILE
INTERNATIONAL
http://www.lmii.com
Tonewood, glue, and finishing supplies.

MC MASTER-CARR
http://www.mcmaster.com/
Bridge saddles, various parts and supplies.

MUSICMAKER'S
http://www.harpkit.com/
Music wire, zither pins, tuning wrenches, tonewood, bows, bow hair, and rosin.

ROCKLER
http://www.rockler.com/
Tools, supplies, glues, wood, and finishes.

STEWART-MACDONALD
http://www.stewmac.com/
Tonewood, glue, and finishing supplies.

SUFFOLK MACHINERY
http://www.suffolkmachinery.com/
"Timberwolf" brand bandsaw blades used in resawing—excellent cut quality.

WOODCRAFT
http://www.woodcraft.com/
Tools, supplies, glues, wood, and finishes.

Index

Lightning Source UK Ltd.
Milton Keynes UK
UKOW07f0240060716

277789UK00004B/194/P